Truth Engine: Applying AI to Investing

Leonidas Tam, Ph.D.

Truth Engine: Applying AI to Investing

This Truth Engine: Applying AI to Investing paperback edition
published 2023

2023 2024 2025 2026 2027 10 9 8 7 6 5 4 3 2 1

Copyright © 2023 Amicus AI Advisors, LLC

All rights reserved.

Leonidas Tam asserts the moral right to be identified as the
author of this work.

A catalog record for this book is available from the Library of
Congress.

ISBN 979-8-9894044-0-7

Epigraph

I do not know what I may appear to the world,
but to myself I seem to have been only like a boy
playing on the seashore, and diverting myself in
now and then finding a smoother pebble or a
prettier shell than ordinary, whilst the great ocean
of truth lay all undiscovered before me.

– Sir Isaac Newton

Dedication

For my daughter

Contents

Contents

Contents

Contents

1 An Unfulfilled Job

It was a sunny day on Wall Street, and the machine was learning. In nearby Long Island, a small group of mathematicians led by an erstwhile Stony Brook department chair implemented what would be wildly successful learning algorithms on market data. While strategies such as mean regression, that a company usually returned to the average of its peers, were widely analyzed, for the first time the strategy could adjust its own parameters. Such automation removed the slow reaction times of human input. Yet in terms of broader impact, Renaissance Technologies' methods fell short. Firms like Citadel torpedoed market liquidity benefits via algorithmic front-running.[1] When Renaissance launched their value fund, the Institutional Equities Fund, it failed to deliver on their expectation. Shortly after creation, the fund dropped 8.7% in the single month of August 2007, and worse a 10% differential with the market.[2] Their ambition of a large capacity value-based fund in the vein of Benjamin Graham and Warren Buffett outran the technology available. Two subsequent breakthroughs in AI would realize the methods for intrinsic value discovery as practiced by the greats, and in the course, empower the individual value investor to conquer markets.

Famed investors Howard Marks, Buffett, and Charlie Munger outline a view of intrinsic value investing that supersedes value investing taught in neat bundles. Their method of investing, even while rooted in valuation methods that hark back to hard and fast rules like Graham's requirements on price to book, goes a step beyond. Buffett has been quoted "Read 500 pages every day".[3] In "The Most Important Thing", Marks writes:

> In fact, one of the things I most want to emphasize
> is how essential it is that one's investment approach
> be intuitive and adaptive rather than be fixed and
> mechanistic.

- Chapter 1, Second Level Thinking

Marks provides the on-ramp for our emphasis – if we're to use quantitative tools in an investing approach, they should be adaptive, generally intelligent methods.

There are many AI doomsayers that say the machine will replace humans. Currently, we know of no machine learning (ML) systems acting on the market that are not intermediated by the designers at some level. Gregory Zuckerman writes that founder Jim Simons pulled the plug on the Renaissance system when drawdown exceeded 20% in a month.[4] When questioned by his lieutenants, Simons gruffly replied, "I would do it again". Simons had built a world-class quantitative team. In balance, we have access to LLMs and generative AI tools that the Renaissance team could only have imagined (fig. 1.1). Yet access to tools is not enough. Equally important is the understanding and experience that elevates the apprentice to artisan.

The Roman philosopher Seneca relates the parable of seeking wisdom from Socrates. In the story, a young man approaches Socrates, then a famed philosopher and leader of the Athens School of Philosophy. "Socrates, I thirst for wisdom. Please give it to me". Socrates makes an appointment with the young man to meet at the River Eridanos at dawn. When they met, Socrates, a burly man, plunged the young man under water and held him there. Finally the young man surfacing and gasping, half assaulted Socrates. Again holding him, Socrates delivered the message, "when you want wisdom as much as you wanted to breathe, you'll attain it." Typically, knowledge isn't equated

Estimated Returns Doubling Time (Rule of 72)

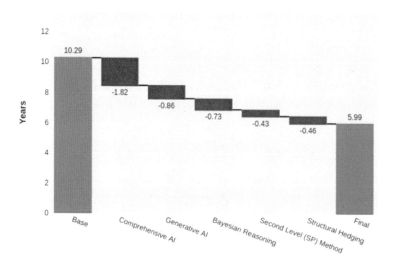

Figure 1.1: Data-driven techniques to improve return, reduces investment doubling time. The techniques require critical thinking and provide a framework for an investor to improve. Like diet and exercise, expected gains vary by diligence and effort.

with wisdom. Socrates had wisdom, for which knowledge is a precursor. Socrates led a school of professionals, which through his dialectic, shaped his teachings. At Nvidia where I worked, the CEO employed the World Wide Field Operations division, essentially a global real-time knowledge collection apparatus. As individual or even professional investors, we likely don't have the resources to build an organization rivaling a Fortune 10 company, yet we have an equal thirst for knowledge as any executive. The argument that investors don't need a world class information apparatus is defeated by Buffett's inspiration to be 15% Philip Fischer. Fischer, active from the early half of the century, made the case for the "scuttlebutt" approach, the practical gumshoe methods of collecting information ahead of broad market discovery.[5] Knowledge and information are the hallmarks of good investment. The promise of new ML tools is that some alchemy of knowledge to wisdom can be shouldered by good systems.

However beneficial, Socrates and his philosophy can be removed from daily professional life. To understand generative AI tools, imagine instead you're a mid-career working professional in software development, who's recently welcomed a junior developer, Earnest. Earnest is good, that's why you hired him, but you know he's green. Further, you're at the peak of your skills—you're pretty sure that you know more than the new guy. But he has such new ideas maybe picked up with recent coursework distilled from the latest studies. The new guy never seems to get the task exactly right, but he really gives it a good effort and sometimes his effort launches a project to the next level. You'll keep him around. Besides, our increasingly multi-disciplinary workplace requires flexible brain power to accelerate time to solution. The power of generative AI is that it applies to the vast majority of knowledge work all at once.

To understand the origin of generative AI (fig. 1.2), we trace ML methods that have already achieved results eluding teams of

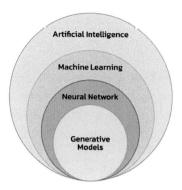

Figure 1.2: Hierarchy of AI technology

elite programmers. The first breakthrough occurred with convolutional neural networks (CNNs) that stacked neural network (NN) layers for deep learning (DL) models. Such models are effective for analyzing visual imagery. CNNs improved the accuracy of image classification tasks, reaching renown in the global ImageNet competition. There is a joke in the pre-DL era that a sophisticated geolocation photo application could be prototyped in a week whereas determining the species of birds in a photo would require a team of world-class computer scientists.[6] During my graduate work, teaching computers to see meant using complex visual flow mathematics, tracking the vector fields between pixel values. Alex Krizhevsky, a researcher at the University of Toronto, ushered a Galilean-scale breakthrough by mastering new computational hardware to implement NNs.[7]

In particular, generative AI uses natural language (NL) as an interface. In mid 2023, the Writer's Guild embroiled the entertainment industry in a strike with generative AI as a core issue. Yet the strikers haven't demanded a complete ban. Since using generative AI is as easy as speaking, there are no wrong ways to use generative AI, only more or less optimal patterns (Chapter

10). Second, NL models have reached par or exceeded human level performance for narrow tasks as measured by the Stanford General Language Understanding Evaluation (GLUE) benchmark.[8] The SuperGLUE benchmark is the second-generation understanding benchmark covering ten tasks including sentiment analysis, entailment (does one phrase imply another), co-reference resolution (was a reference to an earlier mention identified correctly), reading comprehension with common sense reasoning, etc. As most investing texts emphasize a comprehensive and common sense approach, the stage is set for NL and generative AI approaches to create impact in intrinsic value investing.

1.1 Mathematical Complexity Muddies the Waters

ML approaches are not new in intrinsic value investing, and every finance students can appreciate the proto-ML method of least squares to fit a line. Surprisingly, the creator of least squares, the famed polymath Carl Friedrich Gauss used a technique that an intrinsic investor would appreciate to get at the truth of the data. Gauss' famously used least squares estimation when he located the asteroid Ceres, which had been lost in its transit across the sun. Competing against a field of astronomers, Gauss combined least squares regression in a one hundred hour iterative triangulation procedure to minimize and control error. Intrinsic value investing is a time-honored discipline to evaluate prices based on the true value of a company, taking into account both qualitative and quantitative factors. Thus like value investors, Gauss took simple methods applied in a principled fashion to achieve remarkable results. For his achievement, Gauss received the directorship of the Göttingen Observatory.

The limitations of linear regression in dealing with the complex and noisy nature of financial markets led to the development of more advanced techniques. Stochastic calculus emerged as a crucial tool for modeling and understanding the dynamics of financial markets. Stochastic calculus has roots in natural study. In 1827, the botanist Robert Brown observed the random deflection of pollen in water under seemingly the influence of no visible agent. The quantitative physical explanation of Brownian motion formed one leg of Albert Einstein's annus mirablis (miracle year) in 1905, for which he won the Nobel prize in Physics (the other legs being explanations of the photoelectric effect and special relativity). Related to Gauss' idea that deviations are regularly distributed, one of the key concepts in stochastic calculus is the idea of a stochastic process. A stochastic process is a collection of variables with probabilities that represent the evolution of a system over time. The three economists Fischer Black, Myron Scholes, and Robert Merton used geometric Brownian motion (GBM) in their Black-Scholes-Merton model for pricing European options. The GBM models the logarithmic return of a stock price as a Gaussian variable, thereby capturing the "random walk" behavior often observed in the underlying asset.

We all learn the area under the curve approach to calculus, but what if the curve represents singular events? The essential mathematical tool used in the study of these stochastic processes is Ito's calculus, named after the Japanese mathematician Kiyoshi Ito. Ito's lemma, a key result of Ito's calculus, provides a method to find the differential of a function of a stochastic process.[9] In essence, it helps us understand how a financial derivative, which is a function of the underlying asset price, will change as the asset price changes. However, stochastic calculus is not without its challenges. Its real-world assumptions often diverge from actual market behavior. For instance, markets can jump and often shift distributions at the same time. Volatility, instead of being constant as often assumed in GBM, changes over time. To counteract these issues, more sophisticated models have been developed, like the jump diffusion model and the stochastic volatility model. Unfortunately, academic flourish does not imply practical usability. Author Nassim Taleb hammered on the topic of ill-assumed priors for tail risk. Even further European options, as might be deduced, aren't the contracts used in US markets, where the freedom (or danger) of early exercise is ever-present.

While providing the mathematical foundation to quantify and sum the random movements observed in markets, stochastic calculus led many practitioners into a morass of calculation. Applied stochastic calculus reached the heights of hubris captured by the story of Long Term Capital Management (LTCM), depicted in "When Genius Failed". Roger Lowenstein's book emphasizes the human tendency of incorrect assumptions. Eventually, the mathematical community recoiled from baked in assumptions in their modeling.

The next wave of models attempted to tackle tail risk using at least the observation that manias and panics manifested as tightly correlated behavior. These models, such as autoregressive integrated moving average (ARIMA) and generalized autoregressive conditional heteroskedasticity (GARCH), provided more accuracy by handling clustered occurrences of volatility, but still had limitations in dealing with the complexities of financial markets, and needless to say, did not have a deeper understanding of the causal drivers of business performance.

In terms of straight-forward and effective calculation, economist William Sharpe's contributions had the insight to endure, being no more complex than required. His Nobel-prize winning work connected time series volatility with risk. This made him a forefather to both the application of economics to market dynamics and risk estimation. His work laid the foundations for the Capital Asset Pricing Model (CAPM), which is discussed in Chapter 3.[10]

With the advent of powerful computing and continued ML development, useful methods with intelligence emerged. NNs and decision trees allowed for the creation of sophisticated models that could better handle the branching complexity of financial markets. Decision trees, especially ones boosted by parallel processing such as gradient boosted trees (XGBoost), allowed rapid optimal combination of factors.[11] NNs, while heralded as universal function approximations, required complex architecture to move from theoretical to practical performance.[12] What girded ML development was the wisdom that with pure mathematical techniques, it was to paraphrase Richard Feynman, too easy to fool oneself. In ML, the marriage of statistics with data-centric computer science found common cause on the basis of not fooling oneself, as discussed in Chapter 2.

The failure of ARIMA and GARCH to conquer markets draws out a deeper connection of ML competition with investing. Like investors and businesses ever improving, ML competitions are never the same. A survey of recent ML competitions shows seemingly pattern-less results. A specialized technique, fractional max pooling, won a diabetic retinopathy image competition, many-fold ensembling won a chest x-ray competition, and auxiliary segmentation (pixel labelling) models hoisted the champions in a cardiac ejection fraction competition. The innovation that powers each win is intimately intertwined with the secret dependencies of the data. In the case of diabetic retinopathy, fractional max pooling, which varies the view across pixels, finds small lesions on a high resolution image. Many-fold ensembling (sec. 9.4) benefits the chest x-ray domain because chest x-rays draw from such a diverse source of possibilities (there are over 20 diseases that can occur in the chest from physical pneumothorax, bacterial infections, viral pneumonia, etc.). Auxiliary segmentation provided the physical volume estimation required in a robust estimate of ejection fraction. Past performance doesn't guarantee future performance because the present is an ever-improving rhyme. In subsequent chapters, we discuss the "rhymes" that generate effective methods. As it turns out, rhymes are usually intrinsic in nature.

In the "Tao of Munger", David Clark writes, "Charlie is a man who can discuss Charles Darwin's thoughts on evolution, Stephen Jay Gould's thoughts on Darwin's thoughts, Albert Einstein's unified field theory, Walter Bagehot's 1873 treatise on central banking, Isaac Newton and Gottfried Wilhelm Leibniz's development of calculus, Marcia Stigum's voluminous work on the money market, Marquis and Jessie R. James's history of the Bank of America, the conflict between Robert Oppenheimer and Edward Teller over the development of the hydrogen bomb, and E. O. Wilson's theories of sociobiology all in the same breath. He can even quote Mark Twain and Immanuel Kant when the occasion calls for it." We get the sense that Munger invests so he can have more time to read rather than reading to invest. Yet reading broadly at the very least enables the reader to multiply experience and live many lives. In ML, we'll cover the concept of unrepresentative or partial experience. Overfitting, where a model becomes specialized to the training experiences, ultimately leads to poor generalization and reduced performance on new, unseen experiences. To address this issue, the core ML strategies of regularization, cross-validation, and ensemble methods have developed to improve model generalization and prevent overfitting (Chapter 2).

1.2 The Computational Age Enables Machine Learning

Just as investors have certain hours to spend in the day, ML often relies on a computational budget. The timeline of modern ML marks a new computer chip that expands the budget. The Graphics Processing Unit (GPU) powers the parallel computa-

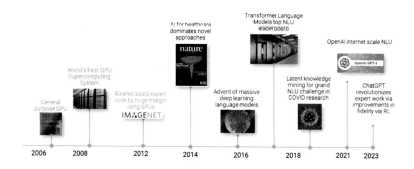

Figure 1.3: Timeline of advances in ML closely correlate to increasing parallel computation performance

tion required to drive the AI revolution (fig. 1.3). Originally, GPUs rapidly manipulated memory to accelerate image rendering into a buffer for output to a display. The architecture of a GPU is designed for parallel processing, which is a type of computation in which many calculations are carried out simultaneously. This is in contrast to a CPU (Central Processing Unit), which is designed for sequential processing. A CPU consists of a few cores optimized for sequential serial processing, whereas a GPU has a massively parallel architecture consisting of thousands of smaller, more efficient cores designed for handling multiple tasks simultaneously.

Stanford researchers Ian Buck, Tim Foley, Mike Houston, and current Stanford Professor Kayvon Fatahalian pioneered the application of GPUs for computing applications circa 2007.[13] Mark Harris, then a graduate student at UNC, coined the General Purpose GPU or GPGPU to describe the tools and usage of the set of programming interfaces that accessed hardware level instructions on the GPU, which Nvidia would rebrand as Compute Unified Device Architecture or CUDA. Nvidia seized on the opportunity to accelerate scientific discovery, a nontrivial investment. The Nvidia founder CEO Jensen Huang invested in CUDA, which not only required a GPU software personnel division, but required silicon area on the chip die. The highly purified silicon chip die forms the surface upon which billions of transistors are etched. The die size is finite and intimately connected with unit costs. Huang commented that the CUDA investment nearly bankrupted the company during the competition with AMD and recession of the Global Financial Crisis in 2008.[14] It didn't help that the scientific computing business unit barely broke even.

The parallel processing capabilities of GPUs have made them an essential tool for DL. DL algorithms perform a massive amount of matrix and vector operations – the kind of calculations that GPUs are designed to handle. By using GPUs, researchers and practitioners can train large NNs quickly, greatly reducing the time needed to iterate. More subtly, GPU applications force designers into a different paradigm of thinking, colloquially described as "thinking in parallel". Every introductory parallel development course starts with the canonical example of accelerating a matrix multiplication, allowing the student to appreciate orders of magnitude (10x) improvement in execution time.

GPUs evolved modern AI because they enabled the use of more complex, larger parameter models that could handle bigger datasets. This led to significant improvements in the performance of ML models, particularly in areas such as image and speech recognition. Thinking in parallel requires NN architecture insight for performance breakthroughs.

1.3 The Pursuit of Scale

In ML, the reductionist premise is larger models and more data generates performance. In short, the approach is scale. As an underlying principle, scale is near and dear to Silicon Valley. It's a somewhat natural idea, albeit requiring significant technical challenges and investments in computational hardware. OpenAI pursued scale with its Generative Pre-trained Transformer (GPT) architectures by collecting internet-scale datasets. The untold technical story is the hand over hand technology ladder climbed by GPU generations in concert with ML frameworks to make full use of their capabilities. Libraries such as CUDA and cuDNN developed by Nvidia provide low-level access to the GPU's parallel computing architecture. At a higher level, software libraries like TensorFlow and PyTorch paved the way for distributed systems, using clusters of computers for supercomputing. Supercomputers paired with OpenAI's drive to chase the trend of scaling to its conclusion led to emergent phenomena. Generative AI could write a rhyming sonnet while acing the LSATs. While OpenAI wasn't the first to pursue scale in computing, with Google Brain running networks as early as 2014 on thousands of CPUs, OpenAI achieved high art through multiplicative ingenuity discussed in Chapter 10. As AI continues to evolve and expand into new areas, GPUs, along with other specialized hardware will continue to play a central role in powering these advancements.

In parallel to these advancements, natural language processing (NLP) techniques were being developed to help investors extract and analyze relevant information from large amounts of unstructured textual data, such as annual reports, financial statements, and news articles. NLP tools enabled investors to identify patterns and trends that may have been previously overlooked, further enhancing their ability to make informed investment decisions.

The introduction of the U.S. Securities and Exchange Commission (SEC)'s Electronic Data Gathering, Analysis, and Retrieval (EDGAR) system standardized capitalism. This system made it possible to access and analyze vast amounts of information related to publicly traded companies. While the standardization of EDGAR systems on the XML format completed in March 13th, 2015,[15] the sheer volume of data available through EDGAR presented a challenge for investors. XML enriches financial filings with meta-data such as CUSIP, balance sheet items, CIK, line item explanations, footnote tags, and thousands more. Search engines such as Google are based on the PageRank algorithm, from Stanford computer scientist Larry Page, that aggregates linking as a signal of quality. Traditional search engines, such as Google, were unable to effectively index and retrieve relevant information from the programmatic databases, where the majority of investment-related data resided.

To overcome this challenge, specialized search tools and algorithms were developed to mine material ensconced in databases for relevant information. These tools, which paired web crawlers with content extraction algorithms, allowed investors to navigate and analyze the wealth of data available through systems like EDGAR. By integrating NLP techniques with these tools, investors were able to extract valuable insights from textual data, helping them identify undervalued stocks and make better investment decisions. The view of large language models (LLMs) as compiled datasets is built on data engineering.

In recent years, the rise of DL and reinforcement learning (RL) techniques has further transformed the landscape of ML, especially as NNs are inherently modular and stackable. RL is a type of ML where an agent learns to make decisions by interacting with an environment over and over again. RL benefited from GPU implementations to achieve state-of-the-art results in complex tasks like playing video games and controlling robots. Some might say RL doesn't quite have the same raw parallel structure encountered in vision and language since decisions are made by interacting with the environment with sequential rewards or penalties. However, it's not completely true since vision and language are core functions of RL agents executed in parallel for counterfactual modeling (sec. 3.8). Advanced RL has been used to develop more accurate and robust models for mortgage pricing, trading execution, and generative AI.

Munger challenges investors to form multiple mental models in order to ascertain factors, such as company management, industry trends, and economic conditions. While quantitative factors can be easily measured and incorporated into models, NL factors often require human expertise and judgment. As a result, creating NL insights overlaps with the holy grail of an artificial general intelligence (AGI). In Chapter 2, we arm ourselves with ML principles that ensure our discoveries really are effective. We add on tools such as cross-validation and a framework for abstractions. In Chapter 4, we build intuition on data, the fuel that powers our engines. We find all data is not built the same and define the boundaries of investigation. In Chapter 5, we'll understand how ML seeks to improve the manual design of heuristic systems. The ML way of thinking incorporates data sources and quality as first-class citizens.

In Chapter 6, we start thinking in terms of systems, which allows us to introduce powerful tools like ReAct and two-stage methods. Chapter 7 consolidates our hard won advances by thinking critically in terms of human decisions and AI interaction. Chapter 8 can now broach the portfolio management question, not merely from a barren mechanical treatment, but in terms of structurally sound approaches. Chapter 9 enters the intermediate stage as we pursue performance through objective function refinement and praxis. Chapter 10 summits understanding generative AI to round out a comprehensive toolbox. We understand how generative AI is trained to better use it and understand when it'll fall short. Understanding it allows deduction of where it'll improve in the near term. Chapter 11 bridges to far term concerns such as AI responsibility and market challenges.

With ever-flowing data streams, the ever-changing nature of financial markets challenges the stalwart value investor. Factors such as market sentiment, government regulations, and macroeconomic events can lead to sudden changes. According to researchers from Stanford Graduate School of Business, ML models give powers to resist bias with the unconventional requirement that they need access to biased factors in the first place.[16] Munger's famed Lollapalooza effect and other cognitive biases must be confronted head on. Using ML, investors can be better equipped to analyze financial markets, identify misvalued companies, and make informed investment decisions. With generative AI accessible to individuals, ML will play an even more significant role in the future of intrinsic value investing.

In the sixteenth century, medical orthodoxy hailed from the teachings of the second century physician Galen. The revered Swiss physician and alchemist Paracelsus sought to disrupt the orthodoxy with radical suggestions such as cleaning wounds and fighting infection. He stood for the primacy of experimental evidence in the presence of increasing resources, trends that eventually ignited the full-fledged Italian Renaissance. In the current sense, we're at the beginning of a journey to forge our own renaissance.

2 No Fooling: Overfitting, Generalization, and TVTP

Investors have a special place in their heart for managers that have skin in the game, whether through equity compensation or stake. Unexpectedly, the Western Canon has enshrined this early. The ancient Arthurian fable of Sir Gawain and The Green Knight expresses the allegory for affluent knights finding their place in the world. When there's not the element of real risk, there's no environment conducive to true learning. On New Year's Day, the strange Green Knight, clad in green from head to toe on a green steed, arrived in court. He challenged anyone to strike him with his axe, under the condition that he will return the blow one year later. The aging King Arthur initially accepts the challenge, but Gawain, the youngest and untested of the knights, steps in to take his place. Gawain beheads the Green Knight with his swing, but to everyone's surprise, the Green Knight springs up. He picks up his own severed head, reminds Gawain of their agreement, and rides off. To make good on his promise, Gawain leaves the comforts of the battlements to brave danger and test his honor. Value investors recognize they truly test their mettle when making a contrarian prediction, and similarly, ML predictive competitions are tests of skill.

To the uninitiated, the alchemy of data appears to come easy with powerful algorithmic tools. ML competitions, where the arbiters withhold evaluation data, separate effective techniques from overzealous ones. The structural conditions that engender powerful ML models are supported by a fundamental understanding of overfitting, generalization, and the train-validation-test paradigm (TVTP). Concisely, the ML designer must promote the learning of general and core principles relevant to task execution while preventing invasion of erroneous correlations that are idiosyncratic. For instance, if a deck of cards had some discernible pattern when dealt, the designer of a general method must focus on the card values rather than say that some of the card backs have picked up wear, lest the pit boss decides to change the decks.

One of the critical concerns in applying ML to finance is model validation to control overfitting. Overfitting occurs when a model learns to perform exceptionally well on the training data but fails to generalize to new, unseen data. This problem can arise when investors use complex models with many parameters or when they don't have enough data to train the model effectively. We can recall the hubris of LTCM when they overfit to the distribution of price movements in the Russian ruble. LTCM only had a heuristic in-domain performance regime. When the Russian currency crisis entered an out of domain regime, it had catastrophic consequences that revealed their bond trading strategy as the proverbial collecting pennies in front of the steam roller. To avoid overfitting, ML practitioners carefully validate their models using techniques such as cross-validation (splitting the dataset into groupings and holding one of the groupings out for testing) to ensure that they have diverse data for training and testing.

High-quality data is the foundation of any successful ML project and investment operation. Unfortunately, financial data can be noisy, incomplete, or inconsistent, which can hamper the performance of ML models. Investors and ML practitioners must carefully preprocess and clean their data sources before feeding it into their models. When utilizing models, it's important to understand the domain and data format used by the model cre-

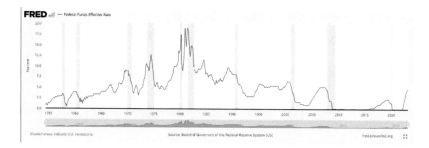

Figure 2.1: The Fed Funds Rate from 1955 to 2023 indicates the central bank interest rate provided to it's member banks. (St. Louis Fed)

ators. In the generative AI age, datasets cover a vast number of domains, and the onus transfers to the user to unlock model performance through Bayesian prompting (Chapter 6.3). They should mind data availability and ensure that data used is representative of the current market conditions, otherwise known as in-domain data use. ML can be used to counter human recency bias, which was brought to the forefront during the failure of Silicon Valley Bank. The management of SVB, while well aware that interest rates haven't historically been near zero, were lulled into complacency with a long run of low rates from 2008 to 2022 (fig. 2.1).

Interpretability and clarity of thought is equally beneficial to scientists and investors. James Clerk Maxwell, the Chair of Natural Philosophy at King's College, London, was a great physicist in a form that rarely exists in modern day. Einstein remarked that he "stood on the shoulders of Maxwell", not Newton. Maxwell famously derived his equations governing electromagnetism in the halcyon days where rigorous theory could spur ingenious experimentation in one person. Maxwell created a complex apparatus for demonstrating knots, due to the way magnetic field lines loop and twist, and even carried string in his pockets to demonstrate knots to acquaintances. The beauty of theory dancing with experimentation comes again with AI systems, and effective use demands such interaction. One of the criticisms of ML models, particularly DL models, is that they can be black boxes with little understanding of how they arrive at their predictions or decisions. DL models exacerbate the issue as they tend to subsume feature engineering, the design of data transformations, in the interest of performance. This lack of interpretability can be problematic when dealing with financial regulations and compliance requirements. Investors must demand transparency and interpretability in their models such that they can refine their theory. For instance, generative AI and and NLU models use attention-based methods that adapt to queries.[17] Shapley value analysis seeks to deduce the marginal contribution of datum to the prediction, allowing experimental ablation tests. Like Maxwell's experiments, ML studies can be tools to reveal invisible forces in a way that might not be clear to the investor at the outset.

Survivorship bias is a logical error that focuses on the remaining subjects in a sample or group and overlooks those that have fallen out of the sample or group. This bias can lead to overly optimistic beliefs because failures are ignored. The World War II airplane example is a classic case study that illustrates this concept.

During WWII, the British Air Ministry examined aircraft lost to enemy fire. They marked returning planes for areas hit by enemy fire. The initial thought was to reinforce these areas since they believed these were the places most likely to be hit during air combat. Areas such as the wings, the tail, and the central body of the aircraft were often riddled with bullet holes. The ministry concluded that these were the areas that needed to be further armored.

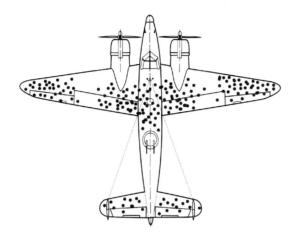

Figure 2.2: Bullet holes in recovered World War II planes after combat sorties *(credit: Cameron Moll)*

However, Abraham Wald, a member of the Statistical Research Group during the war, pointed out a crucial error in this way of thinking – the analysis only considered the aircraft that had returned from missions. It overlooked the planes that had been shot down. Those planes, the ones that didn't make it back, were not random casualties. Wald observed that the bullet holes in the returning aircraft represented areas where a plane could take damage and still continue its mission. Conversely, the areas that were free of holes, like the engines, were likely the places hit on downed planes. These areas were the areas that should be reinforced. In essence, the true story was told by considering the missing, non-returning aircrafts. The correct attribution improved survivability of these planes. Munger would have endorsed the concept of inverting to remedy survivorship bias, commenting "All I want to know is where I'm going to die so I'll never go there".

WWII planes are a little too neat an example compared to

markets. More difficult is to disentangle effects that intermittently pervade the dataset, and to separate fact from spurious correlation. We further investigate survivorship and dataset quality in sec. 6.1. ML designers have addressed sparse rewards through techniques like hard negative mining, selecting hard examples to re-train the network. Even further, we discuss algorithmic rewards in Chapter 10 when reviewing RL and how they're used to align LLMs to societal norms. Societal implications require a careful consideration of omission bias.

ML models can inadvertently perpetuate biases present in the data they are trained on, leading to unfair, unethical, and undesirable outcomes. Investors should be aware of the potential ethical implications of their models and take steps to mitigate any biases in their data or algorithms if they have secondary objectives such as sustainability or moral imperatives. Diversity of thought to promote rigor is better understood when we discuss how Stanford researchers analyze ensembling, combining human and AI judgement (Chapter 9.5). Diversity serves to consider missing or overlooked viewpoints in analysis. It reminds us to question our assumptions, consider all available data, and avoid various omission biases.

2.1 The Train-Validation-Test Paradigm

The Train-Validation-Test Paradigm (TVTP) is a crucial approach for developing effective ML models. The practice embodies physicist Richard Feynman's principle "not to fool yourself – and you are the easiest person to fool". Without a principled TVTP, a prediction contest becomes the proverbial outgoing tide leaving the naked exposed (with methodological flaws). In ML, the TVTP mechanism keeps one covered when the tide leaves. TVTP means splitting the dataset into three parts for analysis – the training set is the bulk at 80% of the dataset, a validation partition at 10%, and testing partition at 10% of the dataset.

Consider the process of studying for an exam. The training set is the study material and practice problems. The validation set includes practice exams to gauge understanding and make necessary adjustments in study strategy. The test set is the actual exam you finally sit for, which evaluates how well you've learned the material. This structure mitigates the risk of overfitting (failure to generalize). By using separate datasets for training and evaluation, one can ensure that the model generalizes well to unseen data. This is especially important when constraints such as time or budget limit the dataset's size. The validation set facilitates model comparison and hyperparameter (model tuning variable) adjustment, while the test set provides an unbiased evaluation of the model's performance on unseen data.

The dataset partitions should be each representative of the source domain. For instance, market capitalization (large, mid, and small) offers a natural heuristic for the investment world. This is a strategy that turns out to be a sensible choice. We discuss further in Chapter 4.

The market mechanism is an evolving contest. Let's take a simple case study of 500 companies, meaning 400 texts for training, 50 for validation, and 50 for testing for the task of identifying buy, hold, or sell decisions. Normally, we train the model using the 400 samples, evaluate and tune the model with the 50 sample validation set, and finally, assess the model's performance using the 50 sample test set. This approach ensures the model is less likely to overfit and provides a reasonable estimation of its performance on new, unseen data. Once a model reaches a level of maturity and is ready to run forward, the model hyperparameters are frozen and the validation set is used for model selection from the ones produced at regular intervals during training.

It's one thing to be familiar with TVTP, another thing to take a fastidious approach. During one competition at Stanford, we encountered the common competition structure wherein participants are given a training set and have the option to access a validation dataset with the penalty of publishing the result to a leaderboard. At the end of the competition, the organizers would perform final evaluation on a test set never released to participants. In our quest for rigor, we maximized our alignment with TVTP by partitioning the training set (80%) into another 90% / 5% / 5% split. This ensures that we never accessed the competition validation set without deliberateness. The expected trade-off for less training data is performance. In the competition, we worked with approximately 70,000 training examples. A large dataset was well-powered to the five categories, and reducing the training set during active development led to approximately a 3% reduction in accuracy performance (fig. 2.3).[18] This was an acceptable tradeoff in order to set us up for underpromising during validation and overdelivering at the final stage. Other competitors weren't so positioned and the final evaluation led to the infamous leaderboard shuffle, the shift in placements showing who was less protected as the tide went out.

TVTP is not foolproof. The pernicious phenomenon of p-hacking can plague TVTP. For instance, an analyst could test the relationship between the future performance of a stock and a multitude of variables such as company size, EPS, market sentiment, past returns, industry sector, and so on. If the analyst performs a separate statistical significance test for each variable, and deems a p-value (statistical significance measure) of less than 0.05 as indicating a significant correlation, they would likely find at least one variable to be significantly correlated with the stock's future performance purely by chance, even if none of the variables truly have any predictive power. As Feynman would remark, they've fooled themselves.

The Bonferroni correction is a method used to adjust for the risk of identifying false positives when performing multiple com-

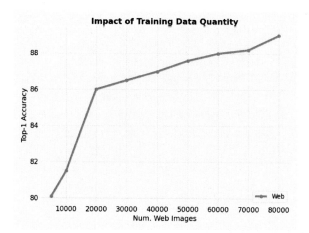

Figure 2.3: Reducing the amount of data available for learning reduces the prediction performance.[18]

parisons, which is often the issue in p-hacking. Bonferroni's correction has an unexpected connection to the Uncertainty Principle – mere observation can change the scientific process. The correction adjusts the significance level (the p-value) by dividing it by the number of comparisons being made. Applying the Bonferroni correction to the above example, the analyst would consider a p-value of 0.05 divided by the number of variables tested (for example, if 20 variables were tested, the new threshold would be 0.0025). This reduces the likelihood of identifying a significant correlation purely by brute iteration. The extra split on the training partition avoids reducing significance due to Bonferroni correction by insulating the evaluation data.

While the Bonferroni correction reduces the risk of false positives, it's a conservative method. It can increase the risk of failing to identify true discoveries, especially when the number of comparisons is large. P-hacking and its correction applies equally to backtesting. Better corrections, such as the iterative

Benjamini-Hochberg procedure, adjust the significance threshold considering related p-values together.[19]

Never let a calculator prevent good common sense from ruling the day. The dataset size constrains the partition sizing, leading to design choices with deep consequences. At Nvidia, I supervised a PhD student who in his ambition to publish insisted on a 95 / 5 /5 TVT split on a dataset of 451 examples (medical data is hard to collect). The student's objective was difficult – differentiate 21 different categories, and he needed all the performance he could eke. Unfortunately, that left only about 21 examples in the test set. My physics thesis advisor Jay Tang always quipped that a new PhD graduate wasn't worth the same as one that had been seasoned in the field. The test set was structurally underpowered to inform performance on all 21 different categories. With 21 random samples across 21 categories, there is one example for each category about nine times in one billion tries. At the very least, cross-validation must be used.

2.2 Cross-validation: Defending Against Generalization Crises

Medical AI faced a serious lapse of faith in 2017. Radiologist Lauren Oakden-Rayner led the critique against over-reaching claims of a physician-beating AI.[20] Even more concerning, the critique, leveled at the dataset and model generalization, rang true. The models, trained on the dataset drawn primarily from the Northeast, failed to generalize well to other parts of the world. Sadly, the developers could've caught their overreach with a simple, yet effective technique. Cross-validation assesses model generalization by utilizing multiple models from one dataset. Let's take an example of making investments based on various features like past performance, company fundamentals, industry trends, and so on. We could collect data for a thousand different

companies over the past five years using identified characteristics, known as features (e.g., P/E ratio, EPS, debt/equity ratio)
that could be important in valuation.

As discussed a way to assess your model's performance would
be to split data according to the TVTP. You'd train your model
on the training set, select the model on the validation set, then
evaluate it on the test set. However, this approach has a downside – it only gives a single estimate of the model's performance.
If the data is noisy or the test set is unrepresentative like the eager graduate student, the estimate could be misleading. Cross-
validation comes to the rescue. The most common type of cross-
validation, and the one we'll use in this example, is k-fold cross-
validation. Here's how it works:

1. Split your data into k subsets, or "folds" (typically, k=5 or
   10).

2. For each round, hold out one of the folds as a test set.

3. Train your model on the remaining k-1 folds, then evaluate
   it on the held-out test set.

4. Repeat this process k times, each time holding out a different fold as your test set.

At the end of this process, you have several measures of your
model architecture's performance. You can take the average of
these estimates to get a more robust idea of how your model is
likely to perform on unseen data. Cross-validation helps make
the most of the data, giving a more reliable estimate of the
model's performance than a simple train-test split. It prevents
overfitting, where the model performs well on training data but
poorly on unseen data. This boosts confidence that the model
will generalize well, producing accurate predictions for companies in the future.

The closest thing humans have to cross-validation procedure is to gather several humans to run an experiment, however even that misses the exact power of cross-validation. In cases where computation is plentiful and datasets limited, developers will use up to ten versions of the model architecture and perform ensembling, a technique described in Chapter 9. The far-fetched human equivalent would be to take ten identical dectuplets, separate and train them in high quality investment programs, and then gather their investment ratings. Cross-validation powerfully replicates a neural network.

2.3 The Nature of Things: Encoders and Decoders

In the world of AI, encoder NNs are detectives that take complex information and boil it down to essential clues. Decoders, on the other hand, are storytellers that take these clues to reconstruct the original or even create something new. Unexpectedly, both have a philosophical intuition reaching over 2000 years ago. Plato's Allegory of the Cave describes a shadow world to illustrate reality and our perceptions of it. Found in Book VII of "The Republic", a group of people have lived chained in a dark cave since birth, never seeing the outside world. They face the wall of the cave and can't look at anything else. Behind them, a fire burns, and between the prisoners and the fire is a parapet where puppeteers walk. The puppeteers, who are behind the prisoners, hold up puppets that cast shadows on the wall of the cave. The prisoners believe these shadows are the real world.

One day, a prisoner is freed. He is forced to turn and see the fire, burning his eyes and bringing longing for days of shadows. He's led outside the cave, and the sunlight again blinds him. Gradually, he adjusts and starts to see the world as it really is. He sees the true forms of the objects, not just their shadows.

The freed prisoner returns to the cave to tell the others about the real world, but the others don't believe him and resist his efforts to free them.

This allegory is a metaphor for the process of enlightenment, according to Plato's Theory of Forms. The shadows on the cave wall represent the world of appearances, which we accept as reality until we discover the world of reality, symbolized by the world outside the cave. The journey of the freed prisoner is the journey of enlightenment, the difficult progression from ignorance to knowledge. The allegory raises various fundamental questions. What is reality? What is knowledge? It touches the role of education and the responsibilities of those who have gained knowledge to share it with others.

The Theory of Forms is also known as the Theory of Ideas, or Platonic ideals. This theory holds that non-physical forms, or ideas, represent the perfect and most accurate reality. In the allegory, the shadows on the cave wall are representations of the physical world as perceived by the prisoners, and this world is a flawed echo of the world of Forms. The shadows are all the prisoners know, much as the everyday objects, ideas, and concepts that people encounter in the physical world are often all they know. Just as the prisoners mistake the shadows for reality, people in the physical world often mistake physical objects, and their imperfect reflections of the Forms, for the ultimate reality.

The freed prisoner, upon exiting the cave and seeing the world outside, is experiencing the world of Forms, the world of the essence of things. When he sees the objects casting the shadows, he's getting closer to the true Forms of things. Neal Stephenson expanded on the concept in his novel "Anathem", hinting at a recursive world of forms, which bridges a connection to Ludwig Wittgenstein's theory of language games (Chapter 10). Rather than biological explanations, philosophical principles explicate how modern AI works.

The Theory of Forms and the study of language is implemented via the encoder NN architecture. The encoder is meant to take the raw sensory data into a conceptual space, a world of Forms. The encoder NN reduces the infinite expression of languages into a tractable numerical space where similar concepts have similar numerical expression. Famously, embeddings allow math with language. The canonical example from Google is a computer system computing King - Queen = Man - Woman. Such conceptual algebra is adapted when an analyst declares the Amazon of China is Alibaba.

The Platonic ideal is natural to investors that live in a meta-descriptive world. Investors determine if the company management conforms more or less to a Platonic ideal of a thriving enterprise. Yet the other side of investing is the ability to estimate business advantages like Buffett's competitive moats. In ML terminology, there is a generative side to investing to produce the investing thesis in the first place. Generative AI uses decoder NN architectures to go from concepts or prompts to instantiations. The intelligent investor masters both encoding and decoding functions (Chapter 10.2).

3 Investing Principles: Margin of Safety and Incompleteness

During the 2023 Stanford Fintech in AI Forum, former credit derivatives quant Ian Osband described developing sophisticated simulators to model market behavior before his manager told him to slot in a constant 20% volatility. If there's one advantage of the intrinsic value investor, the deliberate no-rules rules prevents rigid thinking. The renowned mathematician Kurt Gödel formalized the intuition with his First Incompleteness Theorem, stating that within any given logical system, there are claims that can't be proven true or false using the rules and axioms of that system itself. In layman's terms, within the rulebook of any system, there will always be questions that the rulebook can't answer.

Let's imagine a game of chess. There is a basic rulebook of how each piece moves, who goes first, how the game ends, and so on that can be augmented with strategy. But no matter how comprehensive strategy is, there will be strategic questions it can't answer such as, "What's the best opening sequence?" or "By which turn should castling be accomplished?" The playbook provides the structure for the game, but it can't answer every question about the game.

The connection to investing comes in the acceptance of the existence of questions that can't be definitively answered within a given system designed to answer a specific topic. If one adheres to a rigid heuristic such as a hurdle for gross margin or price to earnings, this assumes that everything can be neatly categorized and understood. However, Gödel's Incompleteness Theorem challenges this perspective by stating that there are always truths that can't be reached merely by operating within a single system.

Thus, to truly grasp the complexity and breadth of the investing world, one must be open to uncertainty, willing to step outside of established systems of thought, and ready to approach problems from multiple angles. Like a chess player who studies both the rulebook and the strategies of other players, we must be willing to engage with the known and the unknown, the definite and the indefinite, in pursuit of understanding. In a sense, Gödel's Incompleteness Theorem raises the importance of intellectual flexibility and humility in the face of the infinite complexities in modern day businesses.

In terms of flexibility, Sharpe's CAPM has a stark reductionism that seems to belie its usefulness. Proposed in 1964, CAPM is a pivotal concept in finance that models the relationship between risk and expected return for assets, particularly public securities. Like the Standard Model in physics that explains three of the four known forces, CAPM serves as a first order framework to understand investment. CAPM postulates that the expected return of a security or a portfolio equals the rate on a risk-free security plus a risk premium. The risk premium is the expected return on the market as a whole, minus the risk-free rate, times the asset's beta. Beta is a measure of the asset's historical volatility as a proxy of risk in relation to the market. CAPM is based on several assumptions, including that investors are rational and avoid risk when possible, there are no taxes or transaction costs, all investors have the same expectations for future investments, and investors have unlimited access to borrow and lend money at the risk-free rate. Under these assumptions, CAPM suggests

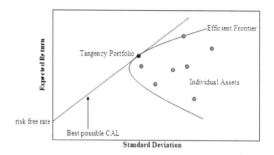

Figure 3.1: The efficient frontier suggests tenable combinations of assets based on CAPM risk-return approximation. CAL = capital allocation line[21]

that the only way to achieve higher expected returns is to accept more risk. The model is widely used in finance for pricing risky securities and generating expected returns for assets given the risk of those assets and cost of capital.

However, CAPM has been subject to various criticisms, primarily around its assumptions violated in the real world, such as the absence of taxes and transaction costs and the homogeneity of investor expectations. Given John Maynard Keynes analyzed concepts such as liquidity preference in "The General Theory", Sharpe as an economist was not ignorant of these concerns. Despite these concerns, CAPM remains a fundamental tool in financial analysis due to its simplicity and utility.

Given a first order estimate of risk and reward, Graham's margin of safety (MoS) concept, with Buffett as an apostle, provides a critical refinement. MoS allows uncertainty to price directly to an action in the present. It forces the investor to immediately make an estimate of the certainty of his investment by converting forward projections into a defense on price. With price, risk, and reward, in dynamic tension, there's already a three variable problem complex enough to occupy any professional assessment.

In physics, even a simple three variable problem such as predicting the orbits of three masses in free space is known to have no analytical (closed-form) solutions.

It's a dirty secret that when analytical solutions failed, scientists relied on iterative estimations, even mechanical ones. To simulate many body gravitational trajectories, light sources substituted for celestial masses. In order to determine the trajectories, scientists would measure the point of maximal illumination on the surface of the spheres from other spheres. That would represent the net pull. They would painstakingly move each mass in proportion to the illumination, which conveniently fell off with the square of the distance just like gravitational forces. By iterating in the tiniest of increments, an accurate trajectory was produced. Nowadays, mechanical models are replaced with GPU-powered simulations that effectively work in the same way resolving the tiniest time step at time. In some ways, investing is estimating an incalculable trajectory from a vortex of factors.

3.1 Business Operations and Margin of Safety

As a classic Buffett aphorism, MoS is simple and works on many levels. It finds unexpected expression in business, in valuation, and in decision-making. Buffett, whom we think of as mainly an investor, has had operational stints. His hands-on involvement with Katharine Graham helming the Washington Post and when he took the reins of Salomon Brothers were notable periods where he exercised business sense in operations. Buffett puts himself in the shoes of managers, and he evaluates managers if they sharply manage businesses as he would. While he prefers businesses that don't require great management, he famously appreciated sharp management when he encountered Rose Blumkin (Mrs. B) and Nebraska Furniture Mart. After selling a majority share to Buffett and forced into early retirement by her family, Mrs. B. proceeded to outcompete the original store with her new store. As any business owner operator realizes, the human capital of the firm forms the first line of defense against competitive conditions. Yet can an investor have an expectation of good management in corporate America?

In a study of employee attitudes at major American corporations, author Stephen Covey uses a soccer team metaphor to bring the situation to life. He wrote of corporate alignment in his book "The Eighth Habit", "If, say, a soccer team had these same [characteristics], only 4 of the 11 players on the field would know which goal is theirs. Only 2 of the 11 would care. Only 2 of the 11 would know what position they play and know exactly what they are supposed to do. And all but 2 players would, in some way, be competing against their own team members rather than the opponent." The power of Covey's metaphor states the need for good managers to corral human resources. Buffett went as far as drawing lines around management, criticizing cost savings campaigns. Paraphrasing Buffett, managers shouldn't wake up one quarter realizing costs are suddenly a factor in operations. Buffett, the manager of managers, prefers fait accompli management. Good management either structurally contains risk or explains the how and why at the same time as the proposed solution to reveal their acumen.

When I was at Nvidia, I had the opportunity to sit in on a meeting with the CEOs of Nvidia and Honeywell, a sprawling conglomerate. The Nvidia CEO Huang said he used mission first management to coordinate disparate actions. In his words, "the mission is the boss". With the mission as the arbiter, coordination and prioritization are streamlined. It's no wonder that a company founder instituted a mission-led culture as startups don't survive without a focused mindset.

MoS has often meant buying at a fair price given a valuation.

Yet how does it reconcile with Buffett's later operandi to buy a good business at a fair price? In a real way, when the evidence stacks up on a good business, it forms confidence. Confidence has a real impact on the investment sizing shown when we analyze expected return. Evidence can be banked as a MoS from increased confidence when allocating finite resources. What are some factors that can build confidence in a company's success?

3.2 The Strange Case of Product-Market Fit

While Buffett often talks about competitive moat, the Silicon Valley ethos of innovation has a curious relationship with competitive moats. The Silicon Valley emphasis on product-market fit over moat unexpectedly connects to the professional consumer unique to established economies. On some level, moat and product are intertwined. A new product will usually have some sort of moat from its newness, affording the company at least time to deepen the moat through standard business tactics. Yet, startups prioritize product-market fit over competitive moat during operations. Startup operations are operational, rubber meets the road affairs, necessitated by the rate of negative cash flow, the burn, prior to profitability. Much higher priority is the concept of product-market fit.

Popularized by Marc Andreessen, product-market fit is how an entrepreneur realizes that the novel product has legs in a market. While described in the trenches as, you'll know it when you find it, product-market fit is when customers start beating down your door for your product in an organic fashion. Surprisingly, it's a concept Buffett probably doesn't need much experience with even as vital as it is in technology. Almost every significant public company (small cap and larger) has achieved product-market fit, such is the bar of entry into the top 1000 companies in U.S. capitalism. As a venture capitalist can relate, product-market fit can lead to dramatic returns. Successful Magellan Fund manager Peter Lynch sketched an everyman approach to recognizing product-market fit in his book "One Up on Wall Street". In his telling, when your kids and all their kids start clamoring for The Limited clothes, they know something the market hasn't heard from the latest 10-Q. The Scottish Late Night Host Craig Ferguson even went so far to identify a professional consumer class targeted by marketers and advertisers, the young. A strong middle class bequeathed a bounty to the next generation for unparalleled resources in education and disposable income. The young consumer is a professional consumer. Startups seeking rapid traction want the approval of a professional consumer. With the imperfection of market earnings drumbeat, market forces don't necessarily gauge product-market fit ahead of earnings. This makes sense as most market participants are professionals that lack a common touch, shrouded in a shadow world of financial analysis. Roman generals on returning from successful campaigns would employ a servant to whisper in their ears that they were only mortal. Fund managers could benefit from such a salutary exercise. Though Munger, with his recognition of value investments such as Costco, seems to have somehow retained the common touch.

Product-market fit is shocking and dramatic, which is the reason no entrepreneur needs to be educated on what it is when it appears. There is a special case that has value investor ramifications, in contradiction to the broad rule that it doesn't affect public markets. Sometimes, an established company launches or refines a product and finds fit in a new niche. The example we discussed is GPUs for AI, which had a 20x effect on Nvidia share price from 2014 to 2020. The Nvidia CEO Huang has the equivalent of Buffett's elephant gun – he seeks to create new business units with $1 billion in annual revenue, which the enterprise division has now handily achieved many times over. The other notable case is the iPhone, which is already entrenched in the popular psyche.

Buffett's avoidance of product fit has perhaps waned. Buffett discussed missing Munger's recommendation of Costco, which has the niche of crave-able high margin items for a middle class clientele. Munger seems to have convinced Buffett. Now Buffett may be philosophically 5% product-market fit. This change may have allowed him to sign off on novel product investments such as Snowflake at Berkshire.

3.3 Dynamic Systems: Overpowering The Limits of Calculation

Markets are dynamic systems, where participants will act on a trajectory in a way that depends on the trajectory itself. We discussed previously the three-body problem, which could suggest that we'd have to abandon all hope of calculation. We don't nearly have any sort of fixed rule like the Law of Gravitation for point calculations on the scale of foreign and domestic markets. Instead we turn to hang our computation on the powerful intrinsic valuation framework.

The reason intrinsic valuation factors bear out is supported quite elegantly, if not simply. Let's dig into the dynamic system problem, which has been known as the self-reflexive problem, a topic physicists originally considered when calculating the trajectory of the electron. In physics, the field model, that charged particles project a spatial temporal map, was developed by Maxwell. Early physicists struggled mightily with dynamic electron models because it wasn't clear in a dynamic field model where the self-field effects would send ethereal particles like the electron. It's really a somewhat miracle that the electron trajectory resolves as elegantly as Maxwell's closed form solution. Self-reflexivity and the path dependence of trajectories, known as hysteresis in electromagnetics, is unfortunately part of market behavior.

Self-reflexive principles require at least a second-level thinking, mentioned by Marks, to consider that if other investors thought like you, what would the market resolve (sec. 3.8). Intrinsic value investing reduces the dimensionality of the problem to a limited number of factors that are self-reinforcing. Intrinsic value investors want other investors to discover their point of view over the sustainable long-term to reward well-managed vital businesses. The additional benefit is that market dynamism can be resolved to a reduced set of tractable factors to be winnowed. Value investors have long used heuristics and screeners to narrow the value factors (in practice we've found 27 especially relevant ones, section 7.2) to a selection, but the not often stated reason is that time is the limiting factor. The complexity of understanding and weighting ever more complex and global businesses with regards to 27 factors in a principled fashion is difficult. Though as Munger urged, buying an excellent business at a fair price can be easier.

Value investing is an established practice, and we're glad to say its effectiveness is alive and well (section 7.2). We've found that subtle combinations of intrinsic factors are recognized by market forces after earnings usually within five trading days. We can take the sign in regular market functioning, the premises of Buffett, Graham, and Dodd are held as correct. Principled investing can overcome market chaos in the long run.

3.4 Mr. Market Is Dead, Long Live Mr. Market

Graham's analogy of Mr. Market, a chaotic manic depressive, is an assistive personification for the investor to resist market gyrations. Will Mr. Market ever rest? A golden age of modern behavioral economics has swept investing for at least two decades, though certainly its roots are deeper (Keynes). Institutional investors are more educated and skilled than ever before. Even more, speculation has found outlet via cryptocurrencies and niche meme stocks. Yet our physical model explains what fluctuations will never go away, playing psychoanalyst to Mr. Market, and how most manager evaluators already know this model intuitively, if subconsciously.

Intrinsic value is a definite contributor to valuations. Let's take a specific example of Nvidia's fiscal 2024 Q1 earnings, where they reported:

- Revenue +19% Q/Q to $7.2B ($670M beat)
- Gross margin 65% (+1% Q/Q)
- Operating margin 30% (+9% Q/Q)
- Non-GAAP EPS $1.09 ($0.17 beat) [22]

Along with a revenue guidance of about $11.0B ($2.9B beat). The most eye-watering figures from their 10-Q are a nine percent increase in operating margin, a ten percent revenue beat, and a revenue guide raise of 35%. The most salient feature is the revenue guide. How could we analyze the impact of an increased revenue guidance on a company's valuation? Here are five standard valuation frameworks:

1. Discounted Cash Flow (DCF): DCF modeling is one of the most commonly used intrinsic valuation methods. It involves forecasting a company's free cash flow (cash flow from operations minus capital expenditures) into the future and then discounting it back to the present using an appropriate discount rate. While not directly using revenue, the calculation of free cash flow begins with revenue, and future revenue growth is a key component of DCF models.

2. Dividend Discount Model (DDM): The DDM is a specific type of DCF model that is suitable for companies that pay

out a significant portion of their earnings as dividends. It involves forecasting future dividends and discounting them back to the present. Like the DCF model, future revenue growth is often an important factor in forecasting future dividends.

3. Economic Value Added (EVA): EVA is a measure of a company's economic profit – the value created above the required return of the company's investors (equity and debt). It's calculated as the net operating profit after tax, minus the cost of capital. Future revenue growth can be important for projecting future EVA.

4. Residual Income Model: This model estimates the intrinsic value of a stock by adding the present value of future residual incomes to the book value of equity. Residual income is earned after accounting for the cost of capital and indirectly impacted by future revenue projections.

5. Revenue Multiple or Price-to-Sales (P/S) Ratio: While less common than earnings-based multiples, revenue multiples can be useful, especially for companies that are not yet profitable or have unique business models. This involves estimating future revenues, then applying a multiple to those revenues based on the multiples of comparable companies.

What would be the impact of a 35% change in revenue on valuation if accomplished? The impact of a 35% increase in revenue on each valuation model depends on factors such as beneficial margin expansion, sustainability of the increased revenue, riskiness of cash flows, and other factors. Here's a simplified analysis of how the 35% increase in revenue might impact each model's valuation:

1. Discounted Cash Flow (DCF): Higher revenue will generally lead to higher free cash flows, all else being equal. If a company's operating margin, tax rate, working capital needs, and capital expenditures stay the same, a 35% increase in revenue should lead to a 35% increase in free cash flows, and hence a 35% increase in the DCF valuation. In reality, these factors may also change with revenue, and the relationship may not be linear due to economies of scale, changes in competition, and other factors.

2. Dividend Discount Model (DDM): If the company pays out a constant proportion of its earnings as dividends, a 35% increase in revenue, assuming constant profit margins, would lead to a 35% increase in dividends and a 35% increase in the DDM valuation. However, if the payout ratio varies or if the increased revenue affects the company's riskiness and hence its discount rate, the impact could be different.

3. Economic Value Added (EVA): If a company's operating margin and capital structure stay the same, a 35% increase in revenue should lead to a 35% increase in EVA, and hence a 35% increase in the company's intrinsic value based on the EVA model. However, as with the DCF model, the relationship may not be linear in reality.

4. Residual Income Model: As with the DDM and EVA models, if the company's profit margin, cost of equity, and book value of equity stay the same, a 35% increase in revenue should lead to a 35% increase in residual income and hence a 35% increase in the company's intrinsic value based on the residual income model. But again, the relationship may not be linear in reality.

5. Revenue Multiple or Price-to-Sales (P/S) Ratio: If the P/S

ratio stays the same, a 35% increase in revenue would lead to a 35% increase in the company's intrinsic value based on this reductionist estimation.

Given that most models expect the price to inflate 35% based on the projection, the 24% change in the present represents a discounted value. The risk premium is 5.75% (11% less 5.75%, the 1 year T-Bill rate). Using Kelly's method, uncovered at the fabled Bell Labs, to calculated the discount yields a probability of success (achieving the revenue guidance, pari passu) of 94.8%.[23] It's a high probability of success supported by Nvidia's track record of execution over the past decade.

We went through the exercise to show that intrinsic valuation really is quite effective. What factors go into the discount then? There is the short-term sentiment, the animal spirits Keynes identified. Then there is the long-term business sentiment, which we distinguish from the roar of the maddening crowd, as operators are too busy executing than to be trading markets (as well as prohibited via regulation).

Mr. Market now seems under the sway of three prevailing winds at any given time. Having a weather vane to estimate each wind would navigate the market. In practice, Buffett tells us we get two for one, the business sentiment and the intrinsic valuation, solely by reading the financial filings (sec. 4.8). Mr. Market's manic depressive episodes may die only to resurface later. The take-home is that good data sources guide long-term investing and promote compounding.

3.5 Metrics, Markets, and Managers

The Financial Industry Regulatory Authority, FINRA administers the Series 65 adviser certification exam as a first step to providing general financial advice to clients, which is further refined by the Chartered Alternative Investment Analyst (CAIA) accreditation for selecting managers. The CAIA explains the unintuitive result that new managers tend to outperform, whereas established managers should always be evaluated for closet indexing, selecting an overly diverse selection that by construction merely replicates index funds at higher fees. While we discuss long short funds (sec. 8.2) where indexing can make sense on the short side, metric-based portfolio selection give a concrete example how simple metric selection such as Sharpe or Sortino ratio has pervasive effects on portfolio behavior.

Having introduced Sharpe earlier, his Sharpe ratio uses the volatility of the security price with respect to market volatility as a proxy for risk. Investors quickly realized that a Sharpe ratio isn't quite what they wanted as it penalized upside variation (when the price moves sharply upward). The Sortino ratio instead only uses downside variation since investors don't mind their investments growing.

When we made the change to substitute Sortino ratio instead of Sharpe ratio, we found that it didn't fit our purposes. The reason had to do with real-life circumstances. Using a Sortino ratio as the supervisory label didn't capture the entire picture for our AI assistant. We had to correct the Sortino ratio to include the timing of dividends. Further, since we target a benchmark, a relative measure against the performance of the benchmark can inject natural hedging. The most disruptive companies often run counter to the market. As we use our AI within our decision process, we want recommendation breadth including possible high returners at the possible cost of path uncertainty. Operational knowledge reveals subtleties that can be lost when theory is removed from exact practice.

3.6 Basic Defense

We touched upon operational decision making, which some managers regard as dynamic hedging. Later we'll discuss how dynamic hedging, updating investments based on best possible information, fits in the framework of Bayesian reasoning. Proactive decision-making is our basic offense, whereas basic defense is required against market forces that mentioned earlier, which are algorithmic agents that seek to take advantage of behavioral fallacies. Given algorithmic market makers sit at firms like Morgan Stanley, established value investors Buffett and Munger give basic defensive strategy to engage in markets rarely. Less action governed by human decisions inexorably means less human error.

Even further defense is to reveal as little information in market action as possible. "Flash Boys" by Michael Lewis investigates the world of high-frequency trading in the US equity market, exposing how certain traders gain unfair advantages using speed and technology. Lewis gave the take-home message that the very order sizing and timing reveals information to exploitative algorithmic agents. Our basic defense is to fight algorithmic fire with fire. Almost all full service, so-called prime brokerages, offer an order type called volume weighted average price (VWAP). VWAP is a benchmark of the average price a security has traded at throughout the day, based on both volume and price. A VWAP order uses a RL trading algorithm to execute an order in line with the VWAP of the security. This strategy was originally used by institutional investors to buy or sell large amounts of shares without perturbing the market price too much. When a large order is placed in the market all at once, it can significantly drive the price of the stock, known as market impact. To minimize this, a large order can be broken down into many smaller orders and executed over the course of a day to align with the VWAP. This way, it mimics regular trading activity rather than a single large trade, thereby disguising the size of the trade. The market sees a steady stream of smaller trades, which is less likely to cause price fluctuations or attract agent attention. The distributed order execution makes it more difficult for other agents to identify the institutional activity, as the trades are spread out and randomized throughout the day. Other market participants, especially high-frequency agents, are constantly looking for signs of large orders and may still be able to infer their presence even when a VWAP strategy is used. In practice, VWAP allows individual investors to move in and out of markets gracefully.

Some prime brokers will offer a rebate for VWAP orders as it provides liquidity to the market with its flexible timing. Better brokers offer a selection of VWAP engines. Like fine wines, some are branded by proprietary firms as they use RL techniques for execution. ML has been in markets and is here to stay. It's only fair to level the playing field.

3.7 Averaging Up

Buffett as the long-term investor found the one strange trick, averaging up, overlooked by global macro wizards and hardcore deep value investors alike. If we are to find an AI method that supports our value investing, it should have characteristics of averaging up, adding to a position even in the face of increasing price. First, what does Buffett say about averaging up or in other words, adding to a position even when it's at a higher prices. As the price increases slightly, he continues to add to his position, such the nature of his elephant gun. Not least are these investments (fig. 3.2):

1. Coca-Cola: Buffett made a significant investment in Coca-Cola in 1988, and continuously added to his position over

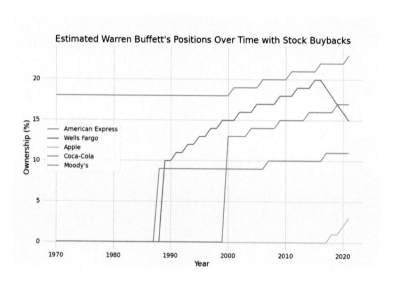

Figure 3.2: Buffett's tendency to average up his ownership and hold for long periods

the years. The company's consistent performance and dominant position in beverages have made it one of Berkshire Hathaway's most substantial holdings.

2. Wells Fargo: Buffett has been a longtime shareholder of Wells Fargo, one of the largest banks in the United States. He started buying shares of the bank in the early 1990s and continued to increase his position over time before disposing of shares in the mid 2010's.

3. American Express: Buffett first invested in American Express in the 1960s, and he has maintained his position in the company for decades. He has been impressed with the company's ability to adapt to changing market conditions and maintain a strong brand.

4. Apple: Berkshire has built up a substantial position in Apple, making it one of their largest holdings. Buffett has been impressed with Apple's management and its strong ecosystem of products and services. Critics that say Buffett isn't a technology investor miss his largest investment.

5. Moody's Corporation: Buffett has been invested in Moody's, one of the leading credit rating agencies, for many years. The company's role in assessing credit risk and providing credit ratings made it an attractive long-term investment for Berkshire.

Further, his preferred method of averaging up is effortless. When his corporations engage in share buybacks, it's especially tax efficient for Berkshire. Just as investors celebrate when managers are able to appropriately reward top employees and retain them, investors should be able to allocate their capital in an accretive manner. We return to the topic when discussing incorporating new information systematically with Bayesian methods (sec. 6.3).

What most don't realize is that Buffett's original investment in Coca-cola in 1988 is an excellent example of a contrarian investment with structural correctness. During the stock market crash in 1987, known as "Black Monday", many stocks were significantly devalued. Buffett saw this as an opportunity. The Coca-Cola Company was one of the world's most recognizable brands, yet its stock price had taken a hit. He started buying shares in 1988, investing about $1 billion in total, which equated to a 6.2% stake in the company.

Buffett realized the strong history of raising dividends rewards the buy and hold strategy. Since that time, Coca-Cola's dividends alone have been enough to cover the cost of the initial investment. Buffett has been quoted as saying that he likes Coca-Cola because it's a simple business that's easy to understand, and it has a durable competitive advantage due to its brand recognition.

When Coke wanted to introduce Cherry Coke into the Chinese market, Buffett even allowed his likeness to be used on the cans for a limited period. He wasn't paid for his endorsement, claiming he was happy to help the company as a significant shareholder. Cherry Coke is his obvious favorite for any who have watched his annual meetings. Berkshire Hathaway still holds its investment in Coca-Cola. As of writing, Berkshire owned approximately 400 million shares, which represents over 7% of all Coca-Cola shares. This makes Berkshire Coca-Cola's largest shareholder, all from a contrarian investment.

3.8 Correctness and Contrarianism

Of late, contrarianism is a prized marketing term, held as universally good, except that without correctness, it's harmful. Researchers from the MIT Sloan School of Management, the School of Economics, and of Cognitive Sciences clarified market relevancy – that surprisingly popular (SP) answers could be correct over the wisdom of the crowd.[24] As a concrete example, they polled a random sample of voters for the question: Is Philadelphia the capital of Pennsylvania? This was a case where the wisdom of the crowd failed.

Their work presents an alternative to the traditional majority voting procedure, which is commonly used for gathering collective intelligence. The authors note that while the wisdom of the crowd is typically superior to individual judgement, the standard democratic voting processes can be biased towards superficial or commonly held beliefs (groupthink), overlooking niche or novel information. To counteract this, they propose an alternative method where the selected answer is more popular than people predict, essentially challenging the usual "most popular" or "most confident" principles. The most confident principle is relevant markets since more confident investors put more capital at risk, whether that belief is correct or not.

The study proposes better decision-making based on a Bayesian model, which calculates a probability by taking into account respondents prior knowledge and new evidence. Respondents vote and rate their confidence in the vote. Their vote predictions fall between two possible worlds – the actual and the counterfactual. For difficult questions (where more people get the wrong answer than normal), the correct answer can be identified as the one that was more popular in the actual world than predicted ex-ante, a SP answer. For example, in the case of Philadelphia, "no" is identified as the correct answer because "yes" is less popular than predicted.

Additionally, the researchers cover a situation where respondents judge the market price of 20th century artworks. Here, the majority vote fails to recognize expensive artworks due to the inherent bias of repeated base rate information factored by each respondent. In this context, the SP algorithm corrects the

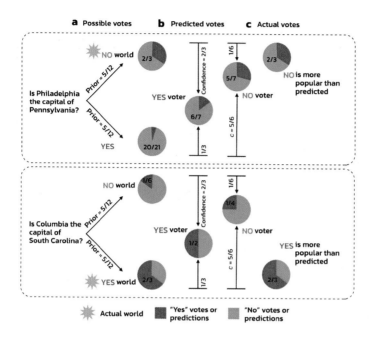

Figure 3.3: The concept of "surprisingly popular" answers is explored using simple models on questions about capital cities. Respondents use Bayesian reasoning to predict what the majority answer will be. The study found that the correct answer to a question is usually more popular in reality than people expect it to be, based on their Bayesian calculations. For example, if yes is the actual correct answer, it will be more popular in the real world than what Bayesian respondents predicted.

majority's bias by reducing the threshold of votes required for an artwork to be classified as expensive.

Further, empirical results from different questions show the effectiveness of the SP method. For instance, on capital city questions, SP reduced the number of incorrect decisions by 48% relative to majority vote. Simulations also show SP's superior performance, with almost infallible accuracy for large samples. However, the method is still dependent on the information available to respondents and their competence. If the available evidence is incomplete or misleading, the answer that best fits the evidence may be incorrect. If some respondents find the prediction task too difficult and default to a 50/50 split or random estimate, it would pull the SP result closer to the majority opinion but not compromise its correct directional influence.

How can we decipher fig. 3.3 in plain English? Both cases top and bottom are framed as Bayesian reasoning. The SP method is a layer on top of Bayesian reasoning. Both the top and bottom are examples where the SP method reverses the wisdom of the crowd (Philadelphia isn't a capital and Columbia is a capital, even though the majority is wrong). We must go through the Bayesian reasoning flow (decide on a prior, update the prior to the conditional distribution, and normalize by the counterfactual world, the so-called marginal distribution). After, we interpolate from our prior to estimate outside the system (what would other people think?). Finally, the difference between the actual votes and the interpolation yields a reversal in the examples. If the Bayesian flow is still confusing, we describe it further in sec. 6.3. Bayesian reasoning isn't the hard part as it's reasonably natural.

The extra work with the SP method has a payoff. The SP method is robust to deviations from ideal (logical) response, and while it has many similarities with prediction markets, it stands apart in its ability to accept non-verifiable propositions. This, coupled with simple input requirements, greatly extends its potential applications. Still, the researchers acknowledge that the SP algorithm is theoretical and its practical success might be limited, depending on how closely actual respondents align with the Bayesian model. Nevertheless, the SP method reduces the bias seen in majority voting, producing more accurate results. It works especially well when there is diversity, a mix of common and unique knowledge among respondents.

How does this work practically in markets? We might think capital markets are not democratic, dominated by a few large firms. Unexpectedly, the US SEC published data on November 2022 on investment firms managing over $100M showing this isn't true. First, there are over 15000 investment firms over $100M with an additional 5500 firms under $100M assets under management, not to mention proprietary firms, both foreign and domestic. In figure 3.4, a bubble plot of the top 200 firms show a reasonable distribution, with three of the top five largest firms being platforms that service other investment advisers. Regardless of the complaints on the concentration of capital (still significant compared to the overall US population of above 300M), the number of asset managers is sufficient for a wisdom-of-the-crowd scenario.

Even with the study's artificial settings, we find elements that match real markets – partial information and participants of varying correctness. In face of uncertainty, we can forge ahead with principles that are contrarian and correct.

3.9 The Problem of Risk

We discussed earlier how risk controls could optimize for the life of the manager rather than total returns. Buffett wages a startling crusade against definitions of risk as volatility, the typical quant definition. Buffett has said, "risk comes from not knowing what you're doing", "the greater the potential for reward

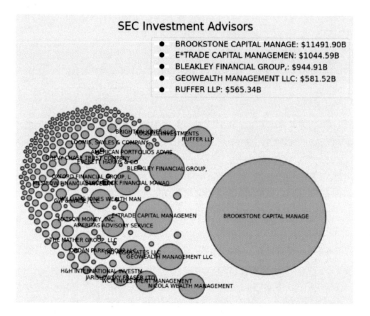

Figure 3.4: The top 200 investment managers with the top 25 labeled. The legend gives the assets under management for the top five firms. The top first, second, and fourth firms are platforms that service smaller managers further diversifying capital management. Data from the SEC retrieved June 2023

in the value portfolio, the less risk there is", and "never invest in a business you cannot understand". The mystery of what's wrong with volatility as risk can be traced to its construction. We even look past the practical insanities where small changes in expected returns can diverge the so-called "mean-variance" solutions based on CAPM. To attack a mathematical construct based on the derived theorems is faulty. William Blake hinted at this when he said, "I must create a system, or be enslaved by another man's". The axiomatic construct of risk as variance admits no business knowledge. It is a theory for the truly lost, which isn't as bad as it sounds. Everyone starts at a tabula rasa for investing with much more unknown than known. The confidence level is poorly calibrated to prediction accuracy. The solution to risk is to learn, to adapt, and to augment.

3.10 Expanding the Circle of Competence

Buffett's risk attribution follows the policy of staying within a circle of competence. In today's competitive and changing world, investing demands we expand the circle of competence in service of returns. Remarkably, it's Buffett's example that suggests the circle of competence is expanded by returning to fundamentals. While Buffett's huge investment in the mature Apple business subsequent to Jobs' leadership is well-documented, we parse Berkshire's investment in Snowflake, an investment that seems to up-end our antiquated conceptions of value investing. Snowflake, as a company, operates in the growing cloud data warehousing sector. Its platform allows businesses to store and analyze data in the cloud, which has increasing demand as more businesses move their operations online, generate more data, and access the data for AI purposes. This fits into the understandable business model preference of Berkshire.

Although Snowflake wasn't profitable at the time of Berk-

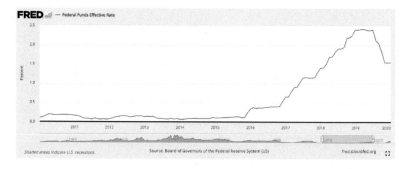

Figure 3.5: The amazing period of low interest rates in the 2010s
corresponded to a period of economic stability, albeit
recovery from the Global Financial Crisis.

shire's investment, its growth potential was evident. Tech companies often take time to become profitable because they invest
heavily in growth in their early stages. Even if the investment
was made by lieutenants Todd Combs or Ted Weschler, and has
the relatively small scale (for Berkshire) of around $1 billion, the
investment derives from Buffett's teachings.

The second piece of the puzzle is the extraordinary period of
low interest rates dominating the 2010's. Stable growth led to
an approximate 511.9% return in a Nasdaq 100 index fund, or an
annualized return of about 19.9%, leading Buffett to analyze low
rates acted like a low-gravity environment. The low gravity of
near zero interest rates allowed top line growth to soar. Missing
out on high growth companies would be a serious dereliction of
duty for any investment manager given the macro environment.

Berkshire personified a learning approach by drawing technology companies into its financial circle of competence through the
lens of interest rates in a modern era. The modern era meaning
a strange new world where low interest rates would normally be
stimulative to such effect that the inevitable tightening would
arrive from Federal Reserve reaction. Berkshire learned a new

language of surrounding the "intangible economy" as described by Imperial College Professor Jonathan Haskel. [25] Undoubtedly the exhaustive reading and study of the Berkshire crew allowed the mastery of techniques to invest in durable high growth.

3.11 The Problem of Track Record

Keynes likened investing to a sort of communal beauty pageant, where the goal is to predict the most popular selection rather than most correct. The value investor sidesteps Keynes' pageantry by measuring over the very long-term and at least selecting those classics that have enduring returns. Regardless, the surprising nail in the coffin for Keynesian pageantry comes through the critical measurement of track record.

Track record, the history of returns of a manager, is the measuring stick and legacy that managers hold up for each other's comparison. What then is the proper length of time to establish a proper track record? Estimates range all over, from an industry standard of five years, from others demanding 20 years for statistical significance, to John Bogel parroting careers are mere coin flips. Bogle repeats the old trope that the investor population is like a zero-sum game where coin flips decides winners and losers. [26] After twenty coin flips, there emerges a one in a million winner through pure chance. First, the observation that markets aren't zero sum over any appreciable growth period would at least reduce this supposition to speculation. Value investors refrain from speculation. More accurately, the mechanistic action of running a portfolio over the long term includes at least thousands of decisions and negative decisions (doing nothing). The successful decisions made by Buffett over his 75 odd year career numbers at least a million. In chess, the number of possible board positions is estimated to be around 10 to the 50th power, depending on the stage of the game. Although this number is mind-bogglingly large, it pales in comparison to the possible decisions Buffett has made over a lifetime. The branching complexity of Buffett's decisions is roughly 2 to the one million, which is 300000 orders of magnitude greater than there are stars in the sky. It's no wonder that chess is now firmly in the rear view mirror of AI, but general intelligence still eludes.

The fallacy is excusable as even physicists sometimes fall into a morass of scale. Some astronomers combined the infinities of space and time to infer the spontaneous assembly of organized structures. Specifically, they posited a fully formed brain, complete with memories of a life like yours, to spontaneously form out of the chaos. This spontaneously-formed brain is known as a Boltzmann Brain, to attack the eponymous physicist for a related theory. In an eternally inflating universe, Boltzmann Brains would be more common than normal brains evolved from stars, planets, and biological evolution. This creates a paradox because it's more likely for us to be one of these random fluctuations (Boltzmann Brains) than the product of a 13.8 billion-year cosmic history. Absurdity comes from poor assumptions, in this case, over assigning chance to sequential events. The coin flip example is a reductio ad absurdum argument.

The only immutable track record is the eternal track record, when the manager's legacy has been laid to rest. As a manager engaging with other managers, the timeless track record convinces. Because scale is so readily attainable in finance, the manager is only as good as his last investment (or inaction). Bezos urged a sort of timelessness at Amazon with his famous "day one" philosophy. The presentness of day one resonates with first principle thinkers. When markets seem almost infinitely scalable to a single man, there's an alchemy at play as described by the Harvard economist Meryvn King. We're still not sure whether the whole edifice will come crashing down. The latest regional bank missteps have animated latent fears. The benchmark achieving growth is the Nasdaq 100, which despite completely excluding financial firms, has demonstrated an exceptional risk-adjusted performance. To put it in the simplest terms, Mark Twain wrote in Tom Sawyer Abroad, "It shows that for all the brag you hear about knowledge being such a wonderful thing, in-stink is worth forty of it for real unerringness". There's a common saying that to err is human, to really screw up requires a computer. The same could extend to finance and leverage. The poor track record of portfolio managers overall, layered with question-able ethics has lead to Buffett praising Bogle. While it seems I come to bury Bogle's caesar, not to praise him, my heart, like Buffett, is in the coffin there with him.

4 Data-Driven Investment: Sources and Quality

4.1 Data Quality: Beyond Garbage In, Garbage Out

You are what you eat. Your investment decisions are only as good as your information. What separates the professional from the retail investor is a serious appreciation for data sources. Whenever I met a geopolitical heavyweight in graduate school (or which there was no shortage at Yale), I would ask what they read regularly. Strikingly, they pointed to the newspapers of record, meaning they didn't have access to special data sources. Initial sources are the major newspapers. Buffett once likened dominant newspapers to toll bridge businesses – everyone looks to the papers of record for a cohesive presentation of current events. We expand beyond the mainstream sources to primary and secondary sources, certainly reviewing the classic business filings such as the 10-K and 10-Q. We'll approximate how much of your time should be spent respectively – information channels are not created equal.

It's well-known Buffett reads voraciously, estimates at eight to ten hours a day are not uncommon. Continuing his 500 pages quote to a collegiate audience, he said, "That's how knowledge works. It builds up, like compound interest. All of you can do it, but I guarantee not many of you will do it." In the modern world, the news feed is near inexhaustible. After analyzing media, our

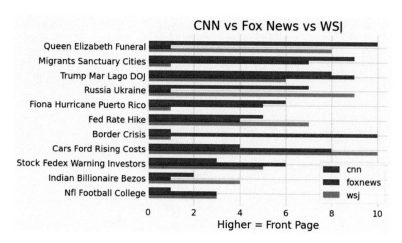

Figure 4.1: A review of political sentiment in major U.S. news outlets[27]

conclusion is that bias and manipulation are rife, even expected. Take even the esteemed papers of record, like the Grey Lady, the WSJ, and WaPo. Bias has been well-characterized (fig. 4.1), but there's more subversive bias beyond liberal and conservative (fig. 4.2). First there are business aims – WSJ falls under the Rupert Murdoch empire. Even with the split between editorial and news, news must still answer to management for business goals. No media company can idle in the fight for readership or viewership. This takes the form of pandering to the audience. The intelligent investor is always on defense for echo chambers. The WSJ print edition naturally targets the entrenched business class on yes, Wall Street, and finance shakers in private equity and corporate mergers and acquisitions. The digital version is different. Take a figure showing the same topic on paper versus digital (fig. 4.2). While the paper readers are the long-standing readership and have scant patience for inflammatory reporting, the digital distribution has a different model. An entire daily

Figure 4.2: Comparison of WSJ digital vs print reporting on similar dates[28]

paper at \$4 a month, the WSJ is targeting full internet viral engagement. It is, after all, a business.

Imagine if you could receive an education from experts in a field actively practicing their craft with an eye on the score. Earnings calls equate to lectures from the best teachers in the industry. The only reason to click on an article versus reading the first hand source is a time constraint. With unreliable mainstream media, reading primary sources is an absolute required investment for the intelligent investor.

Longevity scientist David Sinclair tarnished his reputation when he tweeted a paper on resveratrol containing irregularities such as violations of Benford's Law and insensible physiological correlates.[29] Sinclair should've known better since the paper wasn't from a reputable university or journal. Who is saying it matters as much as what is said, and supports the case for reading primary sources. In business, this is viable as public companies routinely communicate with investors in their investor relations motion.

Let's reason from first principles – is it in their company's best interests to communicate truthfully and wholly with their investors? The question is by itself too difficult to apply to the wide business universe. Let's simplify with a few assumptions and segments, while avoiding absolutes. Take the blue chip companies, which originally meant the twenty Dow Jones Industrial Average companies, by now extended to the top 500 companies by market capitalization. These companies have made it. If you started a company and it's now in the top 500 US companies, it would be worth over \$15 billion, and with the further S&P designation, you have a track record of stability. You've won capitalism and are practically a foundational component of capitalism. If you're even-keeled, it'll be in your best interest to communicate forthright with your investors to reward long-term investment. Likely the business will have some component of stock compensation, which shouldn't fluctuate too widely to affect employee morale. Further the stock price, while shouldn't be a report card on management in the short term, in the long-term it is, as Graham would say, a weighing machine. Long-term investors dislike unexpected surprises one way or the other. We conclude that honesty is in fact the best policy, when running an upstanding business.

On a whirlwind review of Apple's business filings, we noticed their management discussion and risk factors were somewhat terse. There are a few possible reasons for brief communications from a company of Apple's stature. Apple is undoubtedly one of the most closely watched companies. Their every move is scrutinized by legions of analysts and business paparazzi. Like the business celebrities they are, the senior management at Apple has circled the wagons for privacy, not to mention it's in their business culture. Another more cynical view expressed by a mid-market private equity guru is 10-K and Q's have devolved due to legal morass. To paraphrase, when a company does their filings, they get into the room with the lawyers and hash out the maximally legally defensible statements to cram into their filings. Buffett suggests that adding laws on disclosures would reduce the disclosure quality, likely again bringing in the lawyers. Given the somewhat reliable insider's view, is there no information source for candid communication?

Nowadays, any earnings call begins with a reference to the Safe Harbor clause of the 1995 Securities Litigation Reform Act, which comes to our rescue. The topical issue which has been effectively addressed by moving the management discussion to the earnings call. The majority of leadership engages in candid description. They're often exposed to questioning from Street analysts in a sometimes adversarial manner, especially if there have been unpleasant surprises. Another benefit is that the safe harbor opens channels of communication, while tamping down frivolous legal actions. The downside is that the management is under no legal requirement to hold an earnings call, and even if they do as referenced earlier, management is at their own discretion to be just as clamshell as in their 10-K and Q's. In practice, they're likely to limit communication if they've reached the business celebrity paparazzi status, notably business celebrities like Jamie Dimon at JP Morgan reaching that tier or anyone with king or oracle in their moniker. Yet another communication is the shareholder letter, but the letter can often tilt into pure marketing and sales promotion without the quantitative backbone of the quarterly presentation of financial results and guidance that gird an earnings call. Some say the earnings call is less scrutinized as management can freely dissemble. We've noted it's usually what is not said that's informative.

For the earnings call format, typically the operator brings the call online, and then the CEO will give a brief intro and then hand off to the CFO. The CFO, in his best form, will give a by the numbers recitation of the financial statements and key financial metrics. The CFO in best incarnation is the numbers guy, just the facts ma'am. Already our differential analysis engine can rev up – there's been times when the CFO and CEO aren't in sync and figures will undercut forward-looking statements by the CEO, typically in projecting top-line revenue, margin expansion or contraction, or bottom line profitability. It's unavoidable to evaluate the executive team chemistry. A team that is clicking and executing like a well oiled machine is always a pleasure to watch. In opposition, what isn't said is sometimes telling. The omissions are tracked by reading the sector, where challenges affecting an industry like supply chain tightness are broad. Some management teams treat the common investors like how Sergeant Dignam in "The Departed" treats the Feds, keeping them in the dark. Even disdain gives an informational lustre.

After the CFO commentary, the CEO might have a few words or turn it over to the analyst Q&A. Analysts' questioning can vary from friendly to antagonistic. Analysts, while most treat it as a craft to hone, are often beholden to large financial firms that house them for a demand generation function. Thus, some analysts are quite friendly to upward momentum discussion with current management. Further, analysts are tied to the established companies and form a symbiotic relationship. While reasonable, we should be aware of their biases. On the balance, analysts stimulate discussion of especially topical or relevant items. The call concludes often on the hour or soon after with the expectations for the next cadence. Nowadays, there are many sources of earnings call transcripts such that if a delay of five to six hours

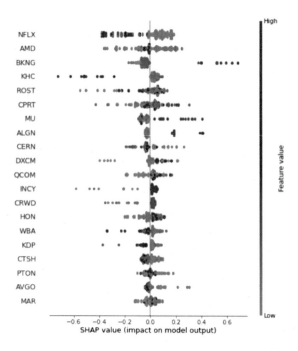

Figure 4.3: Our Shapley value analysis quantifies the marginal contributions of management commentary to the security price. Larger companies have more impactful commentary than smaller ones.

is bearable, the complete day's conference calls, sometimes over 100, can be fetched.

Defying conventional wisdom, earnings calls are better than macro commentary. On September 20th, 2023, both the Fed and Fedex reported. Fedex is a pillar of the economy representing transportation that takes the pulse of the economy. Here are specific results producing actionable content:

Let's take each segment in turn. At FedEx Ground,

first quarter revenue was up 3% year-over-year, driven by a 1% increase in volume and 3% increase in yield. Revenue at FedEx Express was down 9% year-over-year. Volume remained pressured though total Express volume declines moderated sequentially. International export package volumes were up 3% year-over-year. Similar to the fourth quarter, parcel volume declines were most pronounced in the United States.

Across Ground and Express, volumes improved sequentially, aided by the threat of a strike at our primary competitor. We onboarded new customers who valued our service and were committed to a long-term partnership with FedEx. As a result, we added approximately 400,000 in average daily volume by the end of the first quarter and the team did an excellent job focusing on commercial Ground business acquisition...

As you can see on slide 11, monthly volumes have improved sequentially, with Ground and international export volumes inflecting positively on a year-over-year basis. We expect to continue benefiting from this quarter's market share gains throughout the fiscal year. We anticipate improved year-over-year growth rate, especially late in the fiscal year, albeit within a muted demand environment.[30]

From the Fedex results, we get a better sense of dynamic trends. The concurrent growth in international export volumes and Ground point to an ongoing nearshoring trend. Because Freight and Express are muted, this isn't an increase in shipping abroad. Further, we get commentary on labor tightness redirecting volume flows. The actionable content in the call, far above just Fedex, is clearer than the Fed. Of course, the Fed is steering the giant ocean liner that is the American economy. We shouldn't mistake general broad importance with effective information. What about the Fed's labor commentary? Surely, earnings calls can't replace the high level view? We examine General Mills, again reporting the same day.

> Analyst: I have another question on Pet, but not top-line, instead looking at margins. Input costs have been stubbornly onerous for you in Pet, not just you, it seems like the industry at large. The rate of inflation has been a lot higher and for a lot longer. What's driving them? And what's the forward? Like at what point do we start to get some relief there and get to a point where maybe you can get some margin recovery? ...

> Management: We don't expect the operating profit margins to improve this year. As you think about the structure of inflation, some of the same trends that are driving stickiness in human food inputs are there and present, and probably more so on some of the pet inputs, in particular, the conversion costs, which are heavily factored labor [sic], and in particular in the inputs in pet food. So that – until we start to see that trend come off, I wouldn't expect to see any near-term relief on the inflationary pressures on our input basket for pet food.[30]

The General Mills management teaches us about the current state of the value chain and labor inputs for the American food supply. If anything, it's incredible that such information is readily available to the world, such our open society.

The public earnings structure is the core strength of the American market system. The conference call and audited financial statements are pillars to evaluate the sales and go to market strategy. In contrast, the public markets of China don't even come close. Even the American Depository Receipts system, where an American bank or brokerage purchases a large block of shares from a foreign company and deposits them into a custodial account in the company's home country, are at times an end run on domestic audit checks. Even further, our own Shapley value and metrics analysis (fig. 4.3) showed that the top 1000 companies have better filing quality than the next 8000 (the corpus is informative on future performance). Such a result points to the LLM representation as the gestalt of the discourse in a textual corpus. The top 1000 public companies form the core of the American capitalist system. Unexpectedly, the true strength of the American social system extends beyond corporate disclosure into societal discourse, leading to the startling conclusion that GPT-4 could have never been developed in China. We explore the causes and implications further in Chapter 9.

4.2 Understanding the S&P 500 and Nasdaq 100

The S&P 500 and Nasdaq 100 differ in composition and focus. The Nasdaq 100's surprising success originates from effective meta-learning, a desire to continuously improve. Alternatively, the S&P 500 Index is the Hall of Fame of American capitalism. The S&P Index Committee plays the role of gatekeeper, using a detailed selection process. For example, a company must have a minimum market cap of $14.6 billion to even be considered.[31] This is an exclusive club where the bar is set high that only principal components of the US economy may enter.

Beyond financial muscle, the S&P 500 demands that at least 50% of a company's stock be available for public trading. This ensures liquidity to easily buy or sell shares. Companies are US-based (50% of revenue US sourced) and financially stable, and profitable in the last quarter and cumulatively over the last four quarters. The S&P 500 is curated to offer a panoramic view of the U.S. economy, incorporating sectors like technology, healthcare, and consumer goods. Closed-end funds, convertible debentures, exchange-traded funds (ETFs), preferred stocks, rights, warrants, and derivative securities are excluded.

While the S&P 500 aims to capture the essence of the American economy, the Nasdaq 100 takes a more specialized approach. This index is a hotspot for tech and innovative companies, including giants like Apple and smaller, disruptive firms. The Nasdaq 100 is a tech incubator on steroids. The Nasdaq 100 has its own set of stringent rules set by the Nasdaq Index Committee. One rule that stands out is the exclusion of financial companies, which is a strategic decision to focus on sectors with high growth potential and less structural risk. Financial companies naturally have more risk as scale is too readily achieved. Purveyors of risk cater to every C-suite inclination. That the Nasdaq 100 excludes financial companies uncouples from the meta-descriptive life of financial companies. While there are fintech companies in the Nasdaq 100, their products are more likely payment processing with diversified revenue than asset management and loan generation.

When I worked at Nvidia, a top 10 Nasdaq company, there was a pervasive start-up engineering culture direct from the CEO. For instance, the CEO entrusted me with launching the Deep Learning Institute, our global training effort for professionals. With new things, a modest amount of experience and speed of innovation can outpace the field that starts from zero. As Huang would say, "we only want to do the things that are hard, that other organizations cannot do". This atmosphere of innovation aligns perfectly with the ethos of the Nasdaq 100.

The search for exponential growth through new fields is a form of meta-learning policy. While operators remember Toy-

Form of the pages.

	S.	M.	T.	W.	T.	F.	S.
	TEMPERANCE						
	EAT NOT TO DULLNESS						
	DRINK NOT TO ELEVATION.						
T.							
S.	•	•		•		•	
O.	• •	•	•		•	•	•
R.			•			•	
F.		•			•		
I.			•				
S.							
J.							
M.							
C.							
T.							
C.							
H.							
J.							

I determined to give a week's strict attention to each of the virtues successively. Thus, in the first week, my great guard was to avoid every the least offense against *Temperance*, leaving the other virtues to their ordinary chance, only marking every evening the faults of the day. Thus, if in the first week I could keep my first line, marked T, clear of spots, I suppos'd the habit of that virtue so much strengthen'd, and its opposite weaken'd, that I might venture extending my attention to include the next, and for the following week keep both lines clear of spots. Proceeding thus to the last, I could go thro' a course compleat in thirteen weeks, and four courses in a year. And like him who, having a garden to weed, does not attempt to eradicate all the bad herbs at once, which would exceed his reach and his strength, but works on one of the beds at a time, and, having accomplish'd the first, proceeds to a second, so I should have, I hoped, the encouraging pleasure of seeing on my pages the progress I made in virtue, by clearing successively my lines of their spots, till in the end, by a number of courses, I should be happy in viewing a clean book, after a thirteen weeks' daily examination.

Figure 4.4: The Benjamin Franklin meta-learning chart method[32]

ota's kaizen policy of continuous improvement in the Eighties, Benjamin Franklin's method (fig. 4.4) of focusing on one skill at a time to achieve continuous improvement predated kaizen. Just as Franklin systematically improved himself, companies in the Nasdaq 100 are designed to continuously innovate, thereby driving up their values.

The Nasdaq 100 undergoes periodic rebalancing to ensure diversity and prevent over-concentration in a few stocks. For instance, if one company's weight in the index reaches 24%, a rebalancing is triggered. These rules are a safeguard to maintain the index's integrity, much like a gardener pruning the overgrown branches to let the smaller plants flourish. The S&P 500 and Nasdaq 100 are both market-capitalization-weighted indices but serve different purposes.

4.3 Primary Research

Earlier when we discussed Fischer's scuttlebutt methods and Lynch's everyman's edge (sec. 3.2), we touched on the importance of research and primary experience respectively. Primary experience is the unique perspective available to your life path. Inferences on primary experience can risk the trap, "a little knowledge is a dangerous thing". Luckily, just because our experience is limited, it doesn't mean we have to be passive when a confidence level hasn't been met. In fact, it's the very essence of Buffett and Munger's broad and exhaustive reading. Munger didn't just scratch the surface; he delved deep into subjects like general relativity. Primary sources lead to profound understanding. It's one thing to quote physicist John Wheeler "mass tells space-time how to curve, and space-time tells mass how to move", it's another matter to develop the non-Euclidean tensor algebra in combination with rotational dynamics to predict the phenomena of gravitational waves propagating through space-time. When I think the legacy for my daughter, a generative understanding is the most valuable thing to pass to the next generation.

For companies, the best ones go to extreme lengths to deepen their knowledge. In director Christopher Nolan's film, "The Prestige", uncommon magicians enhanced their strengths to the point of incredulity – the strong man disguised as the bent-over elder. At Nvidia, we often "tasted our own champagne", christening each new chip generation by building a supercomputing datacenter for our AI development. Nvidia knows there's no substitute for primary research. The companies providing the best securities analysis software run their own asset management with skin in the game. In Michael Lewis', "The Big Short", analysts traveled to Floridan housing developments to verify defaults in the supposedly safe tranches of mortgage securities. We'll revisit primary research when we discuss model ensembling, examining how it can bolster confidence levels and influence asset allocation strategies.

4.4 The How and Why of Reading

Buffett is serious about reading 500 pages a day, but we don't get the how and why. HBS Professor Clay Christensen tells the story of prompting the legendary Intel CEO Andy Grove to adopt the mantra "only the paranoid survive" when it came to consumer competition. Together, they launched Intel's low cost Celeron processor solution.[33] Grove requested the how from Christensen, and at first, he proffered the middle management approach of forming a new business unit to tackle it. Grove admonished him, saying, "You are such a naïve academic. I asked you how to do it, and you told me what I should do. I know what I need to do. I just don't know how to do it." Grove, specifically wanted the leading metrics and score keeping that could pace the giant to crush the competition. For value investors, it's crucial to establish a systematic approach. The best way we've found is to turn reading into generation.

Value investors think long-term, and that should include the fruits of their reading. A core precept is that we align the output of our work into training data for generative AI. By the natural course of reading filings and distilling insights, we've staged a two-fold improvement. We leave a record for our own investing to promote clear retrospective analysis. Scientists keep a time-stamped laboratory notebook for such purposes. Second, from our notes, we can train generative AI to distill our thinking to force multiply. Our typical recommendation, as we examine later, is to match the text classification task. This means assigning each company a letter grade rating, and then adding a blurb to summarize our thinking. The multi-task approach

Figure 4.5: Micron Technology superinvestor holdings[34]

of classification and summarization aligns with well-established AI methodologies. Now accumulated reading become measurable progress captured by our AI. Accumulating insights from a typical quarter, 60,000 pages and 1,200 companies, produces valuable domain-specific data. It's data that even a leader like OpenAI would be hard-pressed to recreate.

In early 2023, semiconductor Micron appeared among top holdings for institutional investors, even eleven so-called superinvestors (fig. 4.5).[34] The unexpected reason for their misstep can be traced to sector jargon confusing casual analysts. Berkshire avoided the common pitfalls in tech investing that tripped up many experienced investors. Berkshire's defense draws from the circle of competence idea discussed earlier. Buffett avoids the jargon of technology because it can be a trap. Jargon traps finance professionals because the terms form a coded language. Similar words can mean vastly different things. Wittgenstein's writings imply jargon has a purpose.[35] Jargon is how industry professionals communicate business operations.

How is this true of the semiconductor industry? Semis like Nvidia and Micron occupy very different niches on the chip. What may seem cheap for one product is appropriate and expensive for another. The Chairman of TSMC, C.C. Wei cracked,

"I used to make a joke on my customers say that I [make] a few hundred dollars off a chip and then he sold it back to me [for] $200,000."[36] The memory chips that Micron deals are extremely competitive, where the advantage is razor thin ahead of motivated low cost manufacturers. A firm like Berkshire would reject an investment based on the competitive moat. Value investors normally realize the case were it not for jargon obscuring an accurate view. Buffett counters jargon by using his Fischer method of consulting industry insiders, and if they lead him in circles, he knows it's time to walk away. Our firm's technical leadership is bombarded by consultation requests. Our impression is that the high friction consultation process is a detriment to smooth operation. Without being told, industry operators know that Micron memory is somewhat fungible with competitors like SK Hynix, whereas fabrication clients are clamoring at TSMC for their services. That Nvidia has cornered the supply for niche Micron products such as HBM3 memory, which are relatively low volume, adds subtle detail. Even in modern day, Buffett teaches that language and financials must be weighed appropriately.

4.5 Internet Scale Datasets: The Empirical Nature of Knowledge

In our opening chapter, we introduced knowledge and its relation to wisdom. Astonishingly, Berkeley researchers showed LLMs may be community level augmentations revealing latent knowledge.[37] Research scientists are key components in the assembly line that turns facts and experiments into knowledge. The majority of scientific knowledge is published as text and linked charts, which is challenging to understand. This is particularly true in the field of materials science, where machine-understandable data primarily originates from structured property databases, containing only a small fraction of the knowledge in the research literature. Published in the top research journal Nature, a study demonstrated that knowledge from the materials science literature could be encoded into information-rich word embeddings (vector representations of words) without human labelling or supervision. Remarkably, these word embeddings can capture complex materials science concepts such as the structure of the periodic table and structure-property relationships in materials without explicitly teaching chemical knowledge.

Moreover, the study shows that an unsupervised method (just like language modeling) predicted materials for specific applications years ahead of their actual discovery, indicating latent knowledge in the corpus. This suggests that predictive information about near future findings is largely inherent in the corpus. The research underscores the potential of collectively extracting knowledge and relationships from the vast body of scientific literature and hints at a generalized approach to mining knowledge.

The study, which predated modern LLMs, anticipated emergent phenomenon, that is the latent capability that could be revealed with appropriate preparation. Emergent phenomena of generative AI has captured the public imagination, and we examine it in depth in Chapter 10. Datasets fueling modern LLMs are especially rich in conversational knowledge. From the study, latent knowledge emerges from complex, interconnected relationships. In public discussions, it's all too easy to identify single edge cases where an application misses expectation, but that would be missing the forest for the trees. Scientists love quibbling about precedence and knowledge. The AI researcher, Jürgen Schmidhuber, who had vital contributions in recurrent NNs, is the reigning champion of reducing new developments to his earlier works with varying validity. Dismissal of his arguments center around the practical usability of new methods. Generative AI isn't simple information retrieval. LLMs have captured knowledge emerging from conversation at an internet scale. Scientists are well aware of how difficult it is even to know where the conversation is at, usually via in-depth literature review. The essence of large-scale datasets and LLMs lies in their ability to enable comprehensive review and uncover emergent capabilities.

4.6 Knowledge Diffusion: How Information Spreads and Why It Matters

Try this simple experiment at home. Have a friend stand in one corner of the room with a bottle of vanilla while you stand in the opposite corner. The friend uncorks the bottle – why do you almost instantly detect the scent of vanilla? This demonstrates the concept of diffusion, crucial for understanding how information spreads in financial markets. The speed of vanilla molecules reaching you depends on several factors. The difference in molecular concentration, the concentration gradient, the faster the diffusion process. The speed of diffusion generally increases with temperature. Warmer air molecules move more quickly and can therefore disperse a scent faster. Known as convection, the movement of air within the room can speed up the process of diffusion. Larger rooms mean longer diffusion times, all else being equal. The shape of the room could influence how efficiently a scent is dispersed.

Molecular size and mass means smaller and lighter molecules diffuse faster than larger, heavier ones. Auxiliary water vapor in the air can also influence diffusion. In general, scents diffuse more slowly in dry air than in humid air, because water molecules can assist in the transportation of scent particles. Finally, the human detection limit is extremely sensitive at two molecules for every million.

Ultimately, the root mean square (rms) speed provides an average speed for particles in a gas. One could liken it to the average speed of cars on a highway. On any stretch of highway, some cars will be driving above the speed limit, some right at it, and some below. Yet, we can still calculate an average speed that gives us a general idea of how fast cars are going. However, it's not a simple average – it's a little more complex. If we were to take a simple average of speeds, a car going in the opposite direction (which we might think of as having a negative speed) could cancel out a car going the right way. To prevent this, we square each speed before averaging (which makes all the speeds positive), and then take the square root of that average to bring us back to a meaningful number.

The rms speed for vanilla (vanillin molecules) is about 312 m/s. Since the detection limit is extremely low, the high rms speed mean vanilla reaches your olfactory bulb almost instantly. A refinement is that the macroscopic distribution is governed by the diffusion distribution, estimated from kinetic theory using the mean free path, the average distance a molecule travels between collisions, and V_{rms} is the root mean square speed.

The reason we went through an extended analogy is that as investors, we want to be a bloodhound for knowledge and by receiving news at the leading edge, anticipate incoming events. Further, we're interested in knowledge that precipitates wisdom. Business knowledge transmuting into wisdom, as intrinsic value investors know, isn't arbitraged away instantly, as would be the case for high frequency trading front-running a large order block. In our research, we found that knowledge diffusion occurs on the time scale of five days – that is a principled understanding of management business commentary is widely accessed by the community (received at all corners of the room) within five days. In our quantitative methods, the alpha is arbitraged in five days (sec. 11.6). In his book "The Tipping Point", Malcolm Gladwell draws from social research to identify super connectors. We can extend our first principles analysis in his line of thought.

Gladwell's super connectors increase the density of connections similar to concentration of particles. In a community where individuals have many connections with each other, knowledge can spread faster. Just as temperature can affect molecular motion, the availability and efficiency of communication channels (internet, newspapers, schools, etc.) can affect knowledge dissemination. Just as physical barriers can obstruct molecular motion, social, economic, or political barriers can hinder the flow of information. Analogous to the molecular mass, the level and quality of education in a community can affect how quickly new knowledge is understood and spread. Communities with a higher average level of education have the framework to assimilate and share new knowledge more quickly. On a wider level, societal attitudes towards new information, such as openness to new ideas or skepticism of outside sources, can influence how quickly knowledge spreads in a community. In contrast, language barriers can slow down the spread of information, just as varying molecular sizes and masses can affect the speed of diffusion.

In 2023, the social media company X, open sourced the Twitter algorithm. The Twitter algorithm drew rabid interest for those interested in knowledge diffusion. Twitter is an invaluable tool for journalists as they're tasked with identifying information that could diffuse rapidly. The Twitter algorithm works similarly to the k-nearest neighbors algorithm. Like it's name suggests, it tries to show tweets liked or read by a cluster of users similar to the user. The similarity engine of the Twitter algorithm renders the collective consciousness palpable. With the mechanisms of our collective unconscious writ large, it underscores the vital role of the journalist in the fourth estate, the pillar of democratic society. Further, knowledge diffusion connects to innovation. Stanford adjunct Steve Blank described startups as a search for new business models or niches. By its primacy, knowledge discovery precedes new business opportunities.

The oft quoted market adage "buy on the rumor, sell on the news" combines our discussion on primary research and scuttlebutt with knowledge diffusion. Lou Simpson, Buffett's one-time anointed successor, was "in favor of people not knowing what we're doing until the last possible time."[38] One of our successful investments emerged when we sought to access GPUs in the cloud. During early 2023, it became nearly impossible to provision accelerated cloud computing as demand completely overwhelmed supply. We had through our primary experience gained knowledge ahead of management disclosure. Earnings releases represent highly anticipated and covered events where news is disseminated. If following the market adage, it would make sense to release the investment as there's some assurance the value of the insight has been captured by any price movement. On the other hand, the market adage is incomplete as it doesn't address long-term investing. Earlier, we found five days is a far cry from the 90 day disclosure requirement on institutional investors via 13-F filings, though some disclosure encourages long term efficiency.

Understanding knowledge diffusion can inform on trends with a mechanistic explanation instead of platitudes on catalysts and market efficiency. Even longstanding secular trends, the ones that fall under buying a great business at a fair value can fit into the framework of knowledge diffusion, as there's an expectation the market will realize the wisdom of investments and weigh them correctly in Graham's framework.

4.7 The Art of Buying Great Businesses at Fair Prices

Munger advised Buffett to take up buying great businesses at fair prices. Amazingly, the brilliance of buying great businesses at fair prices turns a weakness into strength. Buffett magnanimously lays his minor faults in clear view that we can improve and follow his breadcrumbs. How exactly do we buy great business at fair prices?

One reason is that buying great businesses prevents the investor from sitting on the sidelines too much. Undoubtedly, deploying capital on the whole has helped Berkshire's enormous run starting from the Nineties onward. As Buffett notes, identifying investments has become ever more competitive since when he started in the Fifties. Secondly, the long-tailed nature of returns means sharp spikes occur in the negative and positive direction. By not timing the market, the positive spikes can be captured calmly while the negative spikes should be mitigated by the great business nature. Great businesses at fair prices is buying a hedge in the way a consumer sticks to a strong brand. Buffett had the genius to include in one phrase what takes a discussion to lay out.

When is it best to buy a great business at a fair price? Two clues point to one time – right after earnings. When earnings are announced, we can immediately digest them to determine if it's a great business, according to our intrinsic value metrics. Then, the market reaction to earnings, especially if it's a mild adjustment, is likely to be a current assessment, a fair price. Academics cite market efficiency as if it was a static thing frozen in their sacred equilibrium, but to the value investor and businessperson, time is of the essence. Following from our diffusion discussion, market efficiency is most likely to occur when complete information has disseminated far and wide when the investors are ready to digest it. A great business carries a fair price. Seeking short-term profit contravenes a long-term investment philosophy. Just because there's a cleared market, doesn't mean that all businesses are created equally. Keynes' liquidity preference, which even in the Thirties explained discrepancy in closed-end fund pricing, puts requirements on a security's inclination towards buybacks, dividends, or growth. In the long run there should be no difference, but then again as Keynes says, in the long run we're all dead.

By acting after earnings, whatever scuttlebutt advantage is ceded. Munger's exhortation to play it straight is sometimes best.

4.8 The Market As Signal

Mr. Market personifies the market to deflate its importance and diagnose its manic depression. Though, Graham contends that the market is accurate in the long run, likening it to a weighing machine. How do we reconcile the two comments? In value investing, we take Graham's Mr. Market analogy as fundamentally sound, doubly so with Buffett's endorsement. The premise is that taking the market price as a instructor, isn't well principled. What drives Mr. Market?

The mechanism of Mr. Market is emergent from the socioeconomic crucible. As we hinted at in sec. 3.4, three forces dominate like prevailing winds in meteorology (in physics, vector fields). Many recent experts have identified short term sentiment as influencing prices. As early as Newton's exasperation at "the madness of crowds" to Keynes' "animal spirits", to Shiller's behavioral economics, short term sentiment grips discourse as it is current discourse. The second force is business sentiment. Unlike public opinion, it reflects insiders' expectations and guides over a longer period. When a value investor reads the management's guidance, the discussion and analysis section of a 10-K, they are absorbing business sentiment. Business sentiment is different than short term sentiment as it represents first hand, participatory expectations. We recall our story of the Green Knight that skin in the game engenders the conditions for learning and correct analysis. Without real risk, there is no growth. Counterintuitively, high growth can masquerade as net neutral profit, when managers bet the farm to conquer markets. That business strategy doesn't fit neatly into quarterly cycles presents an opportunity for valuation.

The third force is intrinsic value. When Buffett mentions that low interest rates in the 2010's amounted to removing gravity for valuations, he's acknowledging one of the intrinsic valuation frameworks that incorporate financial reporting. While sentiment can under or overweight a certain amount of growth, at some point growth can become destiny. As the operator's catechism goes, the best way to predict the future is to make it.

At the same time, the market is decoupled from direct action. Early turn of the century physicists recoiled at "spooky action at distance", and likewise the uninitiated regard cleared markets. In a cleared market, no transactions happen; buyers and sellers simply state their intentions through bid and ask (only the so-called specialists with a seat on the NYSE have the uncleared market view, premarket). Further in a cleared market, no transaction need occur for the price (average of the bid ask) to change. All that is necessary is for participants to change their mind simultaneously before the next tick, the next system update. When the market is closed, there is plenty of time before the next tick.

Of the three forces, business operators and intrinsic value investors have the same approach. Huang often describe Nvidia culture as, "we play the game, not the score, because we know if we play the game the right way, the score will reflect it." That's the beauty of Buffett's investor owner mentality. It aligns with the business operators and runs the correct thought process most conducive to learning and improvement. The market as a signal for learning processes falls short for value investors for the same reason it does for business owners. Simpson commented, "I have always felt I could do a better job in adding value by being somewhat removed from the circus and pari-mutuel atmosphere of the market." Only two of the three forces that drive market prices matter to operators that grow long-term value.

4.9 Negative Correlation

Investors often find negative correlations as intriguing as positive gains. While it seems a simple flip to change the evaluation process, the inverse process isn't the same process. To quote Tolstoy, "all happy families are alike; each unhappy family is unhappy in its own way." The same complexity applies to negative correlations in investments. Harnessing negative correlations becomes more difficult because at their heart it's a dissipated phenomenon.

Let's clarify negative correlation with a simple example on company ratings. Consider rating companies using five-letter grade categories. What seems like a simple task quickly becomes a data engineering challenge. Dividing the performance into buckets of say -20% to -10% return and so forth isn't effective (a common error). This regular numerical division leads to an uneven division of companies. Security returns tend to cluster and the regularly spaced buckets will catch much different numbers of companies, a problem known in ML as class imbalance. People instinctively adjust for this imbalance. We can give our learning agents a leg up if instead we divide the companies by quintiles. The saying goes, you're the average of your five closest friends. AI uses a similar logic.

Once the AI is trained with the right data, it can predict which companies fall into different quintiles. Now if we had a 90% certainty of a top grade, it would likely lead to an investment. If instead, we had a 90% certainty of *not* a top grade, now our consideration is spread into four other letter grades. Further, growing economies work against declining asset values in aggregate. At some level, avoiding death in business means building

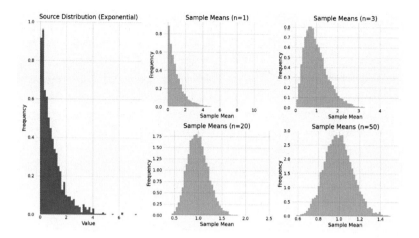

Figure 4.6: Sample means become Gaussian at high samples even when the source is exponential

an institutional resiliency. AI godfather Geoffrey Hinton pointed out that humans face a unique challenge – when someone dies, their knowledge is lost, which isn't true for corporations.

4.10 Even Randomness Has Order

When taking ML into value investing, it's not to throw out the old ways, but to build on sound foundations. Markets have often been described as random walks due to popular literature. As if there was an architect, even randomness has structure. Stanford Professor David Donoho remarks "randomness is too important to be left to chance". When taking a large number of random samples from any population, the distribution of the sample means will approximate Gauss' distribution, also known as the normal distribution. This is a startling result.

With large data sets, whether people, measurements, or scores, it's impractical to examine every single entity within the group. We select smaller groups in a random manner for closer scrutiny. After selecting these samples, we calculate the average values for the variable of interest within each sample. This could be anything from average height and average test score to average weight, depending on the study's focus. These averages make up what's called the sample means distribution.

Interestingly, when enough samples are drawn, the sample means distribution tends to look like a bell curve. This occurs regardless of the shape of the original group's distribution. The normal distribution is characterized by a symmetric, bell-shaped curve and is a foundational concept in statistics.

The unexpected result is why the Gaussian distribution is the "normal" distribution, ubiquitous in nature. The result, known as the Central Limit Theorem tells us that when we take many random samples from a population, the averages of those samples will tend to form a nice, predictable bell-shaped curve, even if the original population's distribution is not normally shaped (fig. 4.6). The normal distribution is like the color brown in a toddler's painting – the color emerges when everything is muddied together. This property is essential in statistics because it allows us to make an assumption to perform calculations with the sample means, making statistical analysis feasible and reliable. The pull of sampling from distributions makes it like a type of gravity.

The other market behavior besides Gaussian behavior is parimutuel distribution. Take a game with several possible outcomes, and everyone can participate by guessing what they think will be the outcome. There's no limit to the number of people who can guess the same outcome. Once everyone has made their guesses, a big pot of prizes will be distributed among those who guessed correctly. However, the prize you receive is not fixed – it's dependent on how many people guessed the same outcome as you. If lots of people guessed the same as you and you're right, the prize gets split many ways, and each person gets a smaller portion. But if fewer people guessed the same as you and you're correct, the prize gets split fewer ways, and each person gets a bigger portion.

Markets are more complicated than simple pari-mutuel games – that's not the statement. Rather, a group of participants can based on the outcomes they've predicted and convincing others, succeed. The participant's reward depends not only on correctness, but also on how many others guessed the same outcome. Thus, outsized rewards accrue to contrarian investors that convince others. Speculators and value investors alike communicate their investments and it isn't good or bad by itself. A durable strategy reflects these constants of markets.

5 Machine Learning Tools for Value Investors

A counter-current in engineering circles cites Apple co-founder Steve Jobs as a manager that didn't understand engineering thoroughly. Unexpectedly, CEO decision-making is informative for AI-guided decision-making. It's true the most epochal decisions Jobs made were at the helm of his second coming at Apple. According to his biographer Walter Isaacson, Jobs had seasoned considerably after missteps with the mixed commercial success of the Lisa and NeXT personal computers. Jobs' maturation, especially at his top-level role as CEO, meant better decision-making. A CEO of a large company is inundated with information and noise. Sorting through the noise and getting to quality decisions is high art. Model ensembling is a quick and widely used way to improve performance in both qualitative and quantitative decision making. Investment committees use manual model ensembling – the leader of the committee listens to the predictions around the table and synthesizes voices into a more accurate decision. Voices with positive predictive value and uncorrelated views contribute most to improving decision making. At Amicus, we developed our own consensus of experts investing copilot to assist with decision making. Gurus such as Lynch and Fischer recommend the individual investor use sources or detective work from their own life experience as viewpoints uncorrelated to Wall Street groupthink. Huang emphasizes the power of diverse groups, holding court with new graduates, technical leads, and vice presidents as equals.[39] As a result, he pivoted the company on a dime, scrapping a bet-the-farm chip project with forward texture mapping with curves for the Riva 128 chip with inverse texture mapping with triangles.[40] Triangle rendering became the future and made his company into a contender. Jobs was famed for his ensembling, often taking a night to mull over insights from his engineers that unsettled him, and then forging a new direction with the often disparate information he integrated.

Previously, we discussed how latent knowledge in datasets pointed to emergent phenomenon. Researchers demonstrated efficient encoding of materials science knowledge from published literature into word embeddings, vector representations of words, without requiring human labeling or supervision. These embeddings are capable of capturing complex materials science concepts, including relationships between material properties and structure.

The insight realizes the power of domain specific analogies and the word2vec algorithm to capture these relationships. Yet there are challenges to adapting this method to generative AI. Namely, how can the scoring methods adapt to a general generative AI?

5.1 A Research Superpower

At Nvidia, a colleague Dr. Barker, a PhD mathematician with roots in the UK Defense Science and Technology Laboratory, the equivalent of the Defense Advanced Research Projects Agency (DARPA) had a superpower. The superpower was in the most unusual of places, at the blackjack table. One evening at the Computer Vision and Pattern Recognition (CVPR) Conference held annually at the Bellagio in Las Vegas, we waited out a restaurant line at the tables. Our senses weren't quite up to the task of card counting, Ed Thorp's widely known high-low technique, and anyways the continuous shuffling tended to break accumulated advantages. Nevertheless, Dr. Barker wasn't one to give up on optimal play at the least.

Blackjack, for the uninitiated, has two main characteristics. Domestically, it's a unidirectional game were all player cards are played face up implying a basic strategy, an optimal action just considering the player's cards. The basic strategy can be modified by the revealed player cards across the table. Second, the house edge is very slight at around 0.28% per hand while the variance is high at 1.28, leading to emotional rollercoasters similar to public markets investing. Dr. Barker used his secret weapon – when flustered, he simply asked the crusty dealer what the optimal action was. In engineering parlance, he consulted an oracle as a cheatsheet for proper action. What form would an oracle for value investing take?

We're considering an engineering oracle as opposed to the Delphic oracle, which in mythic tales rarely led to good strategy. We seek good strategy, not threads that seal the tapestry of our fate, tempt not. In the end, Barker, the trained spy, was disguising the limits of his abilities as he later confided, he was counting cards. Generative AI sometimes behaves like Barker, disguising true abilities until asked. We later understand this through a Bayesian lens.

5.2 Relative Value and ML Classification

In "The Red Queen" by Matthew Ridley, he identified sexual selection for genes as a perpetual race, where competitors press forward just to stay in place. The modern market mechanism has much in common with red-fanged nature and its constant competition. Value investors understand competition intuitively with competitive moats as a first class citizen. Relative value helps us compare competitors directly. In ML, identifying differences through relative comparison is a powerful method. Classification is the ML task of placing inputs into categories. When combined with a percentile division on a metric, learning between competitors is maximized. Numerically, it acts as a form of normalization (fig. 5.1). Normalization, which is placing the companies as a whole on some comprehensible footing, enables discriminative features to shine through noise.

The caveat to relative value and competition is resisting envy. At Nvidia, we had a near paranoid focus on competitors, no matter how small or how difficult it was for new entrants to break into the capital-intensive industry of chip design. Even further, my grad school friend, a former competitive ballroom dancer, identified a Red Queen effect when sizing up the competition during warm-up. She said the competition always is more fearsome during warm-up because there's a natural inclination to doubt ourselves when facing challenges. For business performance, relative value and competitive estimation is a potent mix.

In "The Outsiders" by William Thorndike, he identifies Henry Singleton of Teledyne as an unparalleled CEO and skilled manager of technological investments. Singleton balanced both relative value and invested in new technologies where there was weak competition. Singleton had an uncanny knack for evaluating the landscape of competitive industries, often identifying green fields, untapped markets or niches with low competition but high potential for returns. This allowed him to invest Teledyne's capital in areas where the company could secure a dominant market position relatively easily. His moves were not random bets, but informed investment based on rigorous analysis and a deep understanding of industry dynamics.

Henry Singleton's ability to identify green fields was underpinned by a robust analytical framework that took into account multiple variables, such as market trends, technological advancements, and competitive dynamics. Before committing Teledyne's resources, Singleton would conduct thorough market research to

Aspect	Relative Value	Absolute Value
Interpretability	Harder	Easier
Normalization	Input and output normalized	Requires scaling or post normalization
Outlier sensitivity	Less	More
Domain Knowledge	More required during normalization, less at output	Less during calculation, more at output
Generalization	Better where relationship between variables matter	Worse where relationships between variables matter
Computational Complexity	High if taking AI approaches	Standard computational resources sufficient
Feature Engineering	Some	Usually straight-forward
Use Cases	Better for comparison across sectors	Sufficient for comparison within sectors

Figure 5.1: Comparing relative value and absolute value suitability for ML

understand the size of the opportunity, often leveraging data analytics, expert consultations, and feasibility studies. This helped him pinpoint markets that were poised for growth.

For instance, if Teledyne was considering an investment in a new technology, Singleton would look at the maturity of that technology, its adoption curve, and the potential market size. He would then assess the competitive landscape to see how many companies were operating in that space, their market share, and their technological capabilities. An industry with fewer competitors, especially those less technologically advanced, signaled a green field.

One notable product Singleton oversaw was the Teledyne Ryan Aeronautical AQM-91 Firefly, a reconnaissance drone developed during the Vietnam War era. This high-altitude, long-endurance, radar-invisible drone was designed for surveillance and reconnaissance missions and represented a significant technological advancement in unmanned aerial systems. The AQM-91 Firefly showed how Singleton ventured into specialized markets with high barriers to entry and significant technological demands. It demonstrated Teledyne's capabilities in the emerging field of unmanned systems and solidified its reputation as a technological innovator.

Huang carries the mantle for Singleton. Huang's acquisition of Mellanox, the maker of Infiniband high speed interconnects, displayed prescience that datacenters built for NNs required the fast transmission equivalent of glial cells. These two managers are not impulsive, taking a methodical approach that combines quantitative analysis with strategic foresight. They don't hesitate to divert resources from other areas of the business if there's a green field. By understanding competition and green fields, good management can execute new initiatives for a continuous track record that investors enjoy as enduring businesses.

5.3 Extremely Lazy Yet Exhaustive

Buffett urged that investors be not just lazy in their investing changes, but extremely lazy. How can we reconcile his advice with reading 500 pages a day? Unexpectedly, ML methods can seamlessly fit into Buffett's contrasting recommendations. Clearly, Buffett is not advocating sloth. Similar advice from Nvidia Chief Scientist and Stanford Professor Bill Dally clarifies Buffett's advice. Bill, in addition to teaching us the finer points of HMMA instruction sets, mixed precision inference, and roofline models for L1 and L2 cache access, coached all his research scientists to treat their research ideas like cattle and not like offspring. His advice echoes Nobel laureate Linus Pauling's, "the best way to have a good idea is to have lots of ideas." That way the researcher doesn't get emotionally attached to ideas beyond their intrinsic worth. Operating as a high-throughput researcher means rapidly sorting and refining ideas for ultimate expression. Gauss described this second part as "pauca sed matura", meaning few but mature. The few but mature motto is an investing methodology worth exploring in depth.

The comprehensive AI approach, able to read all the pages of every financial filing, is emerging as table stakes for mature evaluation. Further, research from S&P Dow Jones shows how ranking approaches, where position size doesn't thrash widely, can yield superior returns.[41] The research shows how unexpectedly, ranking is competitive with multi-step optimization. Ranking is generally straightforward and easier to understand. The process is transparent and does not require complex mathematical models or predictions about future correlations between stocks. On the other hand, a ranking-based approach doesn't take into account the relationships (correlations) between different securities to reduce volatility, especially in relation to the market.

Additionally, this could result in a lack of diversification if securities chosen for the portfolio happen to be heavily concentrated in certain sectors or types of companies. The research from the S&P Dow Jones showed that concentration wasn't detrimental as long as the surveyed universe was sufficiently comprehensive – in their case, roughly the top 1000 companies by market cap.

That their empirical study corroborates Buffett's approach towards comprehensive yet lazy action is part of the picture. Buffett, who has been a long-time since running a partnership, rarely emphasized volatility. As mentioned, he prefers to concentrate and average up. Being lazy displaces controlling volatility via correlation as when the position moves against the investor, it becomes an opportunity not a mishap.

5.4 Tool Tradeoffs: Sensitivity and Specificity

Sensitivity and specificity are important descriptors for medical-grade decisions. An understanding of sensitivity (the detection rate) and specificity (the true negative rate) gird a decision framework, and contrarily, the reverse is true. No decision framework escapes sensitivity and specificity. Sensitivity measures how well a test correctly identifies people who actually have a specific condition like a disease. Imagine a group of 100 people, where 30 people actually have the disease and 70 don't. If the test identifies 28 out of those 30 people correctly as having the disease, it has a high sensitivity. In essence, sensitivity answers the question, "of all the people who actually have the disease, how many did the test correctly flag?" (fig. 5.2).

Specificity describes how well a test correctly identifies people who don't have the condition. In the same group of 100 people, if the test correctly says that 68 out of the 70 healthy people don't have the disease, the test has high specificity. Think of specificity

Criteria	Sensitivity	Specificity
Also Known As	True Positive Rate	True Negative Rate
Formula	TP / (TP + FN)	TN / (TN + FP)
Focus	Identifying actual positives	Identifying negative error rate
Interpretation	Fewer false negatives	Fewer false positives
Ideal Values	Close to 1 (100%)	Close to 1 (100%)
Tradeoffs	Boosting may increase false positives	Boosting may increase false negatives
Application	Screening tests	Confirmatory tests

Figure 5.2: Sensitivity and specificity get at different aspects. TP = True Positives, TN = True Negatives, FP = False Positives, FN = False Negatives.

as asking, "of all the people who don't have the disease, how many did the test correctly say were disease-free?"

High sensitivity is crucial for conditions where missing a positive case could have serious consequences (failing to diagnose high-risk cancer). High specificity is important where falsely diagnosing someone as positive leads to waste, like performing an unnecessary surgery and generating anxiety. Ideally, you'd want a test to have both high sensitivity and high specificity, but there's often a tradeoff between the two. Making a test more sensitive might reduce its specificity, and vice versa.

Sensitivity would measure how well your analysis identifies profitable investments. Sensitivity would assess how many of the actual profitable opportunities were correctly identified by your analysis. Analysis with high sensitivity would rarely miss opportunities when a stock is about to go up, ensuring you capture most of the potential gains. However, a highly sensitive analysis might also generate false positives – a static screener on gross margin only considers one point estimate, which is where specificity comes into play.

Analysis with high specificity would help you avoid most of the bad investments, minimizing losses. However, it could be overly cautious and miss out on some profitable opportunities. Given Buffett's "be extremely lazy" recommendation, he endorses specificity.

Buffett has figured out one weird trick for sensitivity and specificity. Use a highly sensitive screening test followed by a high specificity test for action. A highly sensitive analyst adapts valuations as macro conditions change. The specific analyst survives for the long-term as a single high confidence misstep can cost the farm in finance. Like Munger we can invert – the long-term surviving investors are highly specific, just as Buffett suggests they should be. They hunger for more data to confirm their analyses.

6 Data Engineering: Systems Development

Forget the notion that NNs are just another statistical model – statistical models don't force a re-write of your data infrastructure. The key in developing ML systems is that data engineering vertically integrates to systems development. Contrary to first impressions, this both simplifies and complicates processes in the pursuit of performance (fig. 6.1).

In traditional value investing, investors rely on established metrics and indicators like P/E ratios and discounted cash flows to make informed decisions. This manual approach is coded in standard languages and requires constant human oversight. Generative AI is trained on massive financial datasets, guiding them toward your investment goals. Over time, these NNs fine-tune themselves, becoming more effective and efficient decision-making tools. The weights of a network are optimized to fulfill specific goals, such as predicting gross margins, and are generated through learning algorithms like backpropagation and stochastic gradient descent. This shifts the focus of software development to data curation and architecture design.

In traditional software development, human-generated source code compiles into a working binary (computer readable) code. With integrated systems-data architecture, the source code consists of the dataset, training recipes, and NN architecture. Training the network effectively compiles this data into a final, functional NN. Development focus shifts towards dataset curation, a shift that immensely alters software engineering roles and tasks.

106

Aspect	Traditional Software Development	ML Software Development
Primary Focus	Rule-based algorithms	Data-driven algorithms
Code Complexity	High	Low
Data Importance	Low to moderate	High
Model Training	Not applicable	Required
Update Mechanism	Manual patches and updates	Re-training models
Validation	Unit tests, integration tests	Accuracy metrics, validation sets
Output Predictability	Deterministic	Probabilistic
Debugging	Step-by-step debugging	Data inspection, model interpretability
Resource Allocation	CPU, memory	CPU, GPU, memory, bandwidth
Version Control	Code versioning	Code and data versioning
Skill Set	Programming, systems design	Systems, statistics, domain expertise

Figure 6.1: ML development requires a systems-level rethink.

The benefits are substantial – computational homogeneity, parallel batch efficiency, and optimized memory use. It's simpler to adapt, where NN modules inform future architectures with modular reuse. Most importantly, NNs often outperform hand-crafted code in critical applications.

However, the shift comes with challenges. Without additional tooling, models are black boxes. They can fail in unpredictable ways or inadvertently adopt biases from their training data. We use the wandb.ai tools for monitoring hardware and performance metrics. Earlier, we discussed powerful gains arise from substantial curation in financial datasets. Pushing farther, data curation becomes as vital as model architecture, as situational datasets can power thesis-based investing.

6.1 Identifying Key Investment Indicators and Unknown Unknowns

The welcome news is information commoditization extends to financial metrics and ratios. It's now possible to cobble together a bespoke solution from free options. The landscape of data vendors for individual investors is diverse and specialized, tailored to different needs. IEX aims to democratize the stock market, offering comprehensive data on US equities, fixed income, and ETFs, but limited to its own exchange. Quandl, which has discontinued its free stock data offerings, now sells data sets for a one-time fee. AlphaVantage is community-oriented, offering both real-time and historical market data with APIs. Intrinio caters to developers, providing data streams and packets with variable pricing. Zacks offers a holistic approach, featuring real-time and historical data, newsletters, and community involvement. Polygon, a newer vendor, specializes in real-time quotes and data streams and emphasizes community development. EOD Historical Data offers affordability and accuracy. For options data,

CBOE DataShop is a specialized vendor. Interactive Brokers adds another layer to the ecosystem, providing a wide array of trading and data services, including real-time and historical data feeds, as well as APIs suitable for both individual and institutional investors.

On the professional side, Xignite, Thomson Reuters, Bloomberg, and YCharts offer high-end, comprehensive data services, including APIs, real-time data streams, and analytical tools. These are often priced beyond the reach of individual investors, targeting firms and institutional clients instead. Regardless, Stanford researchers point to the "unreasonable effectiveness of noisy labels" in training NNs.[18] This means that NNs are robust to dirty labels, of the sort that would be found in free offerings. It's still up to the user to determine if there's systematic bias or just a random omission in service quality, the latter more common and less concerning in free offerings. The survivorship bias problem continues, as corrected data is a premium feature as well as adding to analysis cost. Sec. 7.2 examines proactive methods to counter survivorship issues. Focus on your objectives despite the noise.

Some say markets are efficient. Others say 10% of active managers outperform the market. The market is Pareto efficient. Making an investment is complicated, and worse timing the market is bad. We outline three techniques to know when there's something amiss. By catching overconfidence and estimating blind corners, we improve our investing.

The Rumsfeld matrix partitions uncertainty quantification into easy chunks (fig. 6.2). Former Secretary of Defense Rumsfeld intuited four quadrants – known knowns, known unknowns, unknown knowns, and unknown unknowns. He singled out the unknown unknowns, UUs for short, as the most dangerous category. The framework has a connection to two business texts – first, Taleb's Black swan events, events that occur at the edge

	KNOWNS	UNKNOWNS
KNOWNS	**KNOWN KNOWNS** OUR CORE COMPETENCIES. INSIDE THE COMFORT ZONE	**KNOWN UNKNOWNS** OUR KNOWN WEAKNESSES. SAFELY AVOID
UNKNOWNS	**UNKNOWN KNOWNS** LATENT SKILLS. READY TO BE DRAWN OUT WITH COACHING	**UNKNOWN UNKNOWNS** WEAKNESSES THAT ARE UNDETERMINED. PRESUMABLY UNHEDGED RISKS

Figure 6.2: The Rumsfeld decision matrix for uncertainty quantification

of the probability distribution with alarming frequency. Second, Rumsfeld was undoubtedly acquainted with "The Art of War", an ancient Chinese text that received wide business scrutiny. Strategist Sun Tzu advises, "know your enemy and know yourself and you can fight a thousand battles without catastrophe". The Rumsfeld matrix is practical. It ties together two aspects of internal and external knowledge to synthesize a useful framework. For the intelligent investor, internal knowledge means a meta-appraisal of the system efficacy while external knowledge is used to appraise the state of market affairs.

We first tackle the external market forces. Knowing where the market is in the cycle could be enormously useful for concentration. In his 2023 annual letter, Buffett stresses that focusing on a few key investments can yield big gains. His methods are paraphrased as "backing up the truck", that is betting heavily when the odds are in favor. The prerequisite for betting heavily is an accurate assessment of the odds for an investment decision. Most organizations focus primarily on external factors. These are the easiest things to discuss with investors or from an individual perspective, easiest to describe on talk shows, pundit spotlights, and dinner parties. The downside is that it's unlikely anybody, from the Fed, to the best executives and economists, know where the aggregate economy is going. Our systems, through its value framework, identifies the simpler cycles of value (section 11.6). Executives and Buffett care more narrowly about business conditions affecting a single enterprise. For intrinsic value investors, careful diligence can uncover such conditions ahead of market discovery.

The much harder predictions are the UUs identified by Rumsfeld. Let's emphasize, the UU's are the number one reason for catastrophe in investing. What are a few concrete UU's. Fraud within a business is a UU, representing illicit activities that are deliberately concealed from investors and auditors. Similarly, unknown geopolitical risks pose a challenge to investments. Even experts like the director of foreign policy studies at Stanford, a former ambassador to Russia in contact with the Biden administration, confessed that the 2023 Ukraine-Russia War was unpredictable. Unknown technological risks add another layer of complexity. Technology has the power to disrupt markets and create novel opportunities. However, only those directly involved in the innovation process – the disruptors on the ground floor – are aware of technological shifts as they occur in real-time. Every engineering manager, former engineers themselves, understands this aspect of genesis when developing new functionality. There is no substitute for the engineer as an individual contributor. Finally, unknown regulatory risks can imperil investments. Regulations are subject to sudden and unexpected changes, making it difficult for investors to anticipate associated risks.

Some of these may seem like regular risks. What makes them a UU? The repetition is a clue. A UU must not only be a risk but must also arise from an unknown source, like a rogue senator becoming a Manchurian candidate.

Now can we take a quantitative approach? With our analysis of UUs, we first understand that a degree of risk is an error bar (range) on prediction. Then the second unknown is actually the fidelity of the error bar itself. That is an unknown source would grow the risk, grow the error bar to an unforeseen degree. Needless to say, most investors don't estimate their UUs because it's difficult. It's difficult enough to even tackle the first degree of unknowns.

During the Berkshire 2023 annual meeting, Buffett unequivocally stated that they never make an emotional decision. Does he really claim to never have emotions and functioning like a robot? More likely, he's achieved high confidence in his decisions that fallacies and irrelevant information are controlled. Similarly, ML classification approaches put out a confidence score with various calibration. This is a general concept that applies as much to autonomous vehicles as it does to securities ratings. There are two primary approaches to increasing confidence scores – Bayesian approaches including Shapley value approaches that measure marginal contributions to risk, and secondly, calibrating the confidence scores themselves, meaning a second level optimization adding more data or models to refine predictions. Hinton spoke to the power of confidence scores for training. In his computer scientist lingo, a rating across 1024 categories is a mere 10 bits of information while adding the 1024 real numbered confidence scores adds 200 times more information.[42] To paraphrase Hinton, when you put your analysis to the test, often times predictions don't work out exactly, and that's why confidence is requisite.

A nice approach from MIT researchers uses a metamodel that strikes one as uncannily human. Their research addresses a significant challenge in ML of making NNs more reliable by better estimating confidence.[43] As discussed, it's not enough for a model to say, "this is a cat". It must say, "I'm 80% sure this is a cat". Traditionally, if you wanted a NN to be good at both making accurate predictions and estimating how certain it is about those predictions, you'd have to train the model from scratch, which is both time-consuming and computationally expensive. This study suggests a more efficient way. Instead of starting from zero, take a pre-trained model – one that is already good at making predictions but not necessarily at estimating its confidence – and add a layer of meta-learning to improve this confidence estimate.

The innovative part is how this additional learning layer is designed. The authors propose a Bayesian metamodel to tweak the existing model in a way that it becomes better at quantifying its uncertainty. They emphasize that this new layer is flexible and can adapt to various situations and applications, whether that involves identifying images that don't fit any known categories. The model can flag potentially incorrect ratings or improve transfer learning, where a model trained for one task is adapted for another. Moreover, the work indicates that a Bayesian layer doesn't require any additional data or structural changes to the existing model. The authors show that their method outperforms existing techniques, providing a more reliable measure of how confident the model is in its predictions.

The MIT technique aligns with our insight – initial model confidence estimates are often too confident. We refine our submodels with a mixture of experts ensemble method (sec. 7), which has the additional benefit of integrating models with different domain knowledge.[1]

---

[1]Rumsfeld's checkered history with phantom WMDs and the Iraq War should be noted. It's possible to become focused on UU's to the point of obsession. The comprehensive nature of our AI prevents fastidiousness from becoming obsession. Decisions should be evidence-based.

6.2 Reasoning AI: The ReAct Method

As we established, estimating unknowns is crucial in both ML and investing for improving performance. Mustafa Suleyman, co-founder of DeepMind, tweeted, "soon, LLMs will know when they don't know. They'll know when to say IDK, or instead ask another AI, or ask a human, or use a different tool, or different knowledge base." Suleyman refers to work published by Princeton and Google Brain researchers in the 2023 International Conference on Learning Representations (ICLR). Their work tackled when generative AI didn't have the right answer at hand. Their technique, called ReAct, combined reasoning and acting (through programmatic interfaces).

The ReAct method expands agent steps to include not just actions that interact with the environment, but also thoughts, which means reasoning in context without producing effects on the environment. These thoughts can serve multiple functions, such as breaking down task goals, applying relevant common-sense knowledge, extracting information from observations, tracking progress, handling exceptions, and adjusting plans.

However, learning in this augmented action space is challenging due to the nearly unlimited possibilities. The method uses exemplars to prompt a LLM to generate both domain-specific actions and free-form thoughts. The model alternates between generating thoughts and actions in tasks where reasoning is crucial (think before you act). In decision-making involving many actions, the occurrence of thoughts and actions is decided asynchronously by the model. It's generative AI reimagined as a warrior philosopher.

ReAct provides several unique advantages. Firstly, it's intuitive and easy to design, requiring human trainers to simply write their thoughts along with the actions they take. Secondly, it's general and flexible, making it suitable for diverse tasks with different action spaces and reasoning requirements. Thirdly, it's performant and robust, showing strong generalization capabilities when learning from up to six in-context examples. Finally, it's human-aligned and controllable, promising an interpretable sequential decision-making and reasoning process and allowing humans to control or correct agent behavior by editing thoughts.

In value investing, you not only execute actions such as analyzing financial statements of potential investments, but also strategize about future moves, like diversifying into different sectors. You may adjust your investment thesis based on new information or market conditions, such as deciding to invest in a different but similarly undervalued company if the one you were initially interested in no longer meets your criteria. Additionally, you seek further information when required, such as consulting industry reports, earnings transcripts, or economic forecasts to better understand the investment landscape.

The method gets AI to do something similar. Instead of just performing tasks or just reasoning about them, the AI does both. It generates a sequence of thoughts and actions, which helps it build, track, and adjust a plan of action. The LLM interacts with external sources like Wikipedia to get more information when needed. The researchers tested ReAct on several tasks, like answering complex questions and verifying facts, and compared its performance to other methods. They found that ReAct was able to outperform other models in a range of scenarios, and that it helped avoid common problems like propagating errors. In learning from reasoned humans, the AI extracts the best from us.

6.3 Closing The Loop

We discussed the remarkable physicist and experimentalist Maxwell. His ability to form an enclosed, original and complete electromagnetic theory stuns those with mathematical, theoretical, or natural appreciation. That he saw so much further than his contemporaries as a mostly solo endeavor stemmed from his completeness to formulate and test his theories with ingenious devices. In his experimental groundwork, he designed the Cavendish Laboratory. Feynman's debunking of mice memory experiments using his sand floor muffling techniques pale at the extent with which Maxwell sought purity in experiments. Equipped with the most precise measurement instruments, Maxwell combined the instruments with the most pristine sound and vibration isolation known at the time.[44] Disentangling interactions in dynamic systems can be mind-bending.

As investors, dynamic systems present a challenge since they bring the difficulty of living systems that change rules. Not only must care be taken to setup pristine experimental environments, such systems must be run forward. Theories are tested forward in smaller scale, which itself is a limitation on behavior. Calculation and record-keeping is kept automatically in a ML framework by logging experimental and dataset input. Retrospective analysis is the equivalent of Maxwell's loop, and anything that can be sensibly done to accelerate closing the loop between experiment and deployment impacts return. Maxwell is noteworthy because he pre-dates the era of big science. One person was able to close the loop between experiment and theory faster than ever seen in physical sciences. Maxwell established the foundations of our understanding of light.

While the halcyon days of closed loop physics are gone (excepting some more experimental domains like MRI physics), computer science offers a new frontier for closed loop investigation. Paired theory and experiment are expected in computer science as experiments are accessible in silico. Stanford scientists used closed loop investigation to probe the shocking behavior of generative AI to take on roles to enhance performance.

Some of our clients expressed shock at our analysis of prompting generative AI to "think like Buffett". After we published results on May 4th 2023, researchers from the Max Planck Institute hit upon the same approach in their May 24th paper, "In-Context Impersonation Reveals Large Language Models' Strengths and Biases".[45] Why would such a simple method be powerful and what's the mechanism that explains why this isn't a slight of hand? Researchers from Stanford University explain mechanisms in their 2022 paper "An Explanation of In-context Learning as Implicit Bayesian Inference" for LLMs.[46]

What is Bayesian inference and why is prompting as Bayesian inference a powerful concept? Prompt engineering is dismissed as obvious to the point of not rising to the level of engineering. Rather, it's taking a simple idea seriously. We'll understand why generative AI requires our intelligence as the value investor to synthesize high performance.

Bayesian inference (reasoning) is a statistical method that combines prior beliefs with observed data to produce updated beliefs. Named after Thomas Bayes, an 18th-century mathematician and theologian, Bayes' theorem is the core principle. The theorem describes how to update the probability for a hypothesis as more evidence becomes available (fig. 6.3). While this general description seems like how human learning and decision works, the power comes in the mechanisms of the prior, the posterior, and the marginal probability distributions in Bayes' theorem.

To explain Bayes' theorem, take the case of evaluating a particular company. The prior is your initial belief about the stock's potential for profit, based on factors like its financial health, market position, and historical performance. This is the best estimate given the limited data you have.

Next, imagine coming across a new quarterly report for the company. The likelihood or update distribution is how well this new information aligns with your belief that the stock is a good

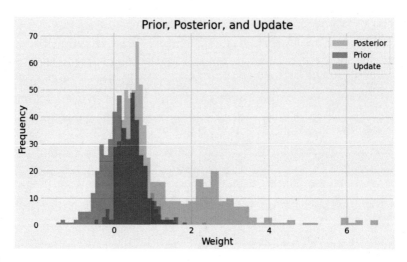

Figure 6.3: We demonstrate our AI-generated Bayesian likelihood update (green) to a market allocation (red) generates a more concentrated portfolio (blue).

investment. A report with increased revenue and reduced debt would boost the company's perceived value. On the other hand, if the company has reported declining profits, it may suggest the stock isn't a good investment.

The posterior is your updated belief about the stock's value after accounting for this new piece of information. If the quarterly report was favorable, your belief in the stock being a good investment would likely increase. Conversely, a poor report would decrease your confidence in the investment. You would then use this updated belief as your new prior the next time you evaluate another piece of information about the stock.

The marginal is trickier and accounts for the broader market conditions and the performance of other companies in the same sector. The distribution normalizes your belief about the stock, ensuring that your investment thesis is not overly focused on this single stock without considering other market variables. This is much like how probabilities should sum up to one in a well-calibrated investment strategy.

In essence, Bayes' theorem is a systematic way of updating your beliefs in light of new evidence. It balances how strongly you believed something initially (the prior) with how much the new evidence supports it (the likelihood), to arrive at a new, updated belief (the posterior).

Bayesian inference has gained popularity in recent years due to its flexibility in modeling complex scenarios and its ability to incorporate uncertainty explicitly. It can handle everything from simple parameter estimation to complex hierarchical models and ML tasks. We tradeoff Bayesian inference versus simple frequentist (one-off) estimation when there's an expectation of longitudinal evidence, like a long-term investment.

We had mentioned Bayesian reasoning is somewhat intuitive, changing expectations based on new information. As Keynes chimed, "When the facts change, I change my mind. What do you do?" Yet Bayesian reasoning can be weaponized. The consultant Jordan Belfort mentions a sales tactic that forces a Bayesian update on his target. When his target declined his advances, Belfort would ramble. Paraphrasing, "well take the situation where I'd been making money for you reliably. If I gave you this stock tip after making money for you for a year would you turn me down? No? Exactly, we would be off to the races making money. So why not put in a small amount now to get started?". In Belfort's setup, he sets up a counterfactual Bayesian update. In fact, he hasn't helped his client. For such abuses, the SEC censured Belfort from the securities industry in 1999.[47]

On the reputable side, Stanford researchers deduced that asking LLMs to take on roles imparts an update distribution to the AI. According to Stanford researchers, LLMs are using Bayesian inference to perform in-context learning. A bloody example from military history reminds collaborators how important it is to draw from the same distribution. During the American Civil War, Confederate General Lee ordered General Ewell to take Cemetery Hill at Gettysburg "if practicable." Ewell, differing from Lee's aristocratic upbringing, didn't follow what was meant as an imperative. The Union later fortified the position with artillery, proving decisive. If Ewell had better in-context learning, an appropriate action may have resulted. The Stanford paper suggests in-context learning updates the probability for a correct response as more context (the user prompt) becomes available. The model infers the underlying concept or pattern from these examples. The more examples they're given, the better they can infer the right answer. While that seems straight-forward, LLMs know something about almost everything, and in-context learning is crucial to usability.

Now there's a wrinkle in out-of-distribution (OOD) prediction decisive to the investing setting. Take the longitudinal setting of adjusting forecasts. While you might have a wealth of information on how the stock has behaved in the past market conditions, it's important to recognize that the market itself is a dynamic entity that can shift due to a multitude of factors. Just as you may have been trying to predict the outcome of a game based on past statistics, the rules of the game can change, affecting the outcome. However, a seasoned value investor will not solely rely on past performance to gauge future returns. Instead, they will delve into the core fundamentals of a company – like earnings, debt, and market position – to make well-informed estimations about future performance. This is analogous to understanding the rules of various games deeply enough to make educated guesses on how changes in rules could affect outcomes. The researchers acknowledge this challenge – the prompts given to the model (predict the next high performing sector) come from a different distribution than the data the model was trained on (past successful sectors). It's like trying to predict a bear market when your entire life has been a bull market.

The researchers provided a mathematical proof showing that, despite lacking OOD information, the model's predictions can still be optimal, as long as each prompt gives enough information about the underlying concept.

To validate their theory, the researchers created a synthetic dataset called GINC with two main components – entities (eg. Maxwell, Newton) and properties (eg. nationality, education) for studying in-context learning. They observed that larger models and longer examples improved the accuracy of in-context learning, providing more evidence that these models are indeed learning through a process like Bayesian inference. For their case, they triggered in-context learning just by conditioning on a prompt that contains input-output examples, without any explicit retraining. The authors explain how this type of learning can occur, especially when AIs utilize long-range coherence.

The researchers hypothesize that the LLM infers a latent document-level concept, which helps to generate coherent output. Then, during the testing phase, the LLM infers the shared latent concept between the examples in a prompt, facilitating in-context learning. This process can occur despite a mismatch between the distributions of prompts and pre-training data. However, they also found open questions and phenomena that aren't yet explained by their theory. This brings us to our current topic, the surprising practice of asking LLMs to impersonate roles (fig. 6.4). Researchers from Max Planck wanted to know if LLMs could pretend to be different roles effectively and if these roles could change how the models approach different problems. To do this, they used a range of different tasks, like the multi-armed bandit problem and reasoning tasks.

Let's unpack the multi-armed bandit problem. Picture a game with multiple slot machines (also known as one-armed bandits), and you can choose to play any one of them on each turn. Each machine gives different rewards, but you don't know which one is best. You need to decide whether to stick with the machine you're currently playing (exploiting) or try a different machine (exploring) in the hopes of getting more rewards. The researchers asked the LLMs to pretend they were people of different ages playing this game. They found out that models pretending to be children explored more, while those pretending to be adults exploited more. The AI had retained the beginner's mind appropriate for new settings.

Now, how did this apply to reasoning tasks. They placed the AI in a game show with different questions. Some were about STEM topics, others about Humanities. The experimenters asked the generative AI to answer questions while pretending to be experts in different fields. They found out that models pretending to be experts in a specific domain did better than those pretending not to be experts.

The researchers also used different models, including Vicuna and ChatGPT-3.5-Turbo. They wanted to check if different models performed differently in these tasks. Finally, they found that when LLMs pretend to be different characters, they can bring out some biases encoded in them. For instance, when pretending to be different races or genders, the models performed differently in some tasks, revealing possible societal biases they had learned.

The research shows LLMs can effectively pretend to be different personas and that these personas can influence their performance and behavior in different tasks. The research helps us understand more about how AIs learn and behave. Yet still the robustness of in-context learning is still a significant challenge. This is because the performance of in-context learning can be highly sensitive to context. This instability means that its performance can vary dramatically, sometimes performing at state-of-the-art levels, and at other times performing no better

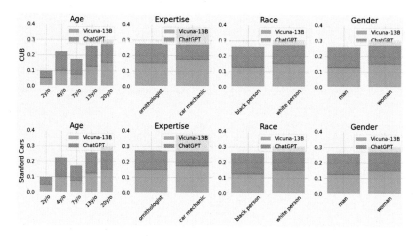

Figure 6.4: When LLMs were asked to impersonate different roles, their performance on various tasks changed, indicating conditional bias.[46]

than random guessing. This is exactly what we explored in our series of analyses of ChatGPT for value investing (sec. 10.11). The Stanford study showed that more labels per class improve in-context learning. Unusually, another Stanford Professor Chip Heath, claims human learning functions in much the same way, as the more contextual clues act as hooks into our memory.[48] Unsurprisingly, the neural architectures in LLMs show a greater capacity for in-context learning than vanilla statistical models.[49]

6.4 Consistent Conceptual Frameworks

Generalization and OOD performance are the crux of AI. Value investors understand strong principles allow weathering all markets, and AI reveals the same through consistent conceptual frameworks. Conceptual frameworks have powerful effects and Cambridge University researchers investigated OOD performance.[50]

The article found LLMs internalize consistent definitions more than inconsistent ones. In fine-tuning on a specific data set, the NN applies gradient updates on neurons corresponding to consistent definitions rather than inconsistent ones. This is described as out-of-context meta-learning, where the network anticipates that consistent definitions will be more beneficial for reducing future training loss, so it internalizes them more.

The authors perform an entity attribution experiment, asking models questions about a variable's name, its meaning, what it stands for, or who it represents. They evaluated the model on these questions after every epoch of a two-stage setup, finding that consistent entities are internalized stronger than inconsistent ones. Their smaller models had weaker internalization with a more challenging dataset.

The research discusses potential mechanisms responsible for weak and strong internalization. A technical hypothesis proposes that gradient descent methods favor gradient alignment across mini-batches. Another study verified the stronger hypothesis that LLMs store factual information as a space-time world model and retrieve these definitions to answer questions.[51]

The paper hints at implications, such as the possibility of LLMs acquiring situational awareness and the potential of RL agents seeking power. The authors suggest that these scenarios need better understanding for proactive measures against potentially harmful consequences. LLMs are capable of out-of-context meta-learning, which could have significant implications for our understanding of foundational models. All this points to LLMs behaving like prodigies – in ML speak, the model has great inductive biases (innate learning propensity). Like a prodigy, AI can learn in leaps and bounds. The benefit for advanced investors is legacy. Your investing analysis becomes a precious resource to influence your generative AI.

6.5 A Data Strategy: Data Monetization

By now, we've examined impressive feats that can be accomplished with data. We now show that data is quantified with dollar figures, and the operational intricacies of your business are a substrate for lasting value. The online social forum Reddit kicked off the data wars. In an announcement that got their user community frothing, they announced access pricing at up to $20M, killing off their third party developers.[52] Estimates suggest Reddit is monetizing at $2.40 per user per year, above their current $1.40 average. Why would they precipitate such a momentous change? The answer of course has to do with AI and ChatGPT. In AI forensics we follow the data trail – how surprisingly, it's revived the fortunes of another Silicon Valley unicorn.

Conversational data, the kind found on Reddit, is the enriched ore mined by OpenAI for generative AI gold. OpenAI writes about GPT-2 and ChatGPT, showing exactly what sources they used for an early version of ChatGPT in fig. 6.5:

> "We scraped all outbound links from Reddit, a social media platform, which received at least 3 karma. The resulting dataset, WebText, contains the text subset of these 45 million links."
>
> "3 million posts from reddit.com across a variety of topics (subreddits), as well summaries of the posts written by the original poster (TL;DRs)... We then re-parse the [Reddit data] carefully using a set of heuristics..."
>
> -- OpenAI[53;54]

The subsequent hand labeling of vast quantities of Reddit data has been a boon to Scale AI, a company that crowd-sources labor for data clean-up. In OpenAI's words, "Our labelers consist of

Subreddit	# posts	% of dataset
relationships	63324	54.3%
AskReddit	15440	13.2%
relationship_advice	8691	7.5%
tifu	7685	6.6%
dating_advice	2849	2.4%
personalfinance	312	2.0%
Advice	2088	1.8%
legaladvice	1997	1.7%
offmychest	1582	1.4%
loseit	1452	1.2%
jobs	1084	0.9%
self	1048	0.9%
BreakUps	838	0.7%
askwomenadvice	688	0.6%
dogs	638	0.6%

Figure 6.5: An early version of ChatGPT used purely Reddit data.[53]

contractors hired either through Upwork, or sourced from Scale AI"[55] Scale and OpenAI have an existing relationship dating to Y Combinator days. Rumors suggest Scale has locked down the data contract from Google's generative AI competitor, Bard. Scale, which laid off of 20% of its workforce in 2023, is allegedly rehiring fired workers with the hard-earned experience from the OpenAI work.[56] OpenAI no longer discusses its dataset practices. In fact, OpenAI has hardened their AI against questioning, even when probing on open source datasets like The Pile, collected by Eleuther AI.

The Pile follows and enhances the initial OpenAI dataset.[57] The Pile includes raw Reddit data of "uncompressed text across 69,547,149 documents", or the equivalent of a human writer writing for 44,000 years or about 733 lifetimes (about 36000 copies of "The Complete Works of Shakespeare"). Considering that OpenAI was already at 45M documents in 2019 and The Pile reached 69M in 2020, OpenAI has likely scaled up to maximum coverage. Reddit reported about 430M daily active users in 2019, which implies about 7.85 billion posts per year.[58] This leaves significant headroom for OpenAI to scale up their API usage.

Data is the new currency in the world of AI. From Reddit's data monetization strategies to OpenAI's massive data collection efforts, we see the direct financial implications of leveraging quality data. Companies like Scale AI capitalize by offering specialized services in data cleaning, which is crucial for building more efficient AI models. The future of this sector hinges on how organizations manage their data – whether they keep it closed or make it open-source. The open source dataset The Pile includes PubMed Central, ArXiv, GitHub, FreeLaw, Stack Exchange, USPTO, Ubuntu IRC, Wikipedia, HackerNews, YouTube subtitles to give a jump start on nearly ever knowledge work domain. With an estimated billions of posts generated yearly on platforms like Reddit alone, the potential for scaling up AI's data requirements is immense. As data collection and management become increasingly sophisticated, its financial impact on the AI industry is bound to grow.

7 Brains Combining Models and Metrics

During the Cuban Missile Crisis of 1962, President John F. Kennedy found himself at the apex of human decision-making, amidst a cauldron of conflicting advice, data, and consequences. U-2 spy planes had returned with irrefutable evidence of Soviet nuclear missiles in Cuba, just 90 miles away from American soil. Kennedy's military brain trust argued for immediate airstrikes to neutralize the threat. Diplomats and advisors, another cognitive subset, urged for negotiation and peace talks. The data (reconnaissance photos, military readiness scores, diplomatic cables) were examined and re-examined, each telling a different story, each pulling the President in a different direction.

Here, Kennedy faced a decision-making environment not unlike that which value investors often find themselves in. He was in a complex, rapidly changing situation that had layers of interconnected consequences. Kennedy opted for a third way – a naval blockade of Cuba to prevent further military supplies from reaching the island, buying time for negotiation. This was neither an outright act of war nor an acquiescence to Soviet aggression. It was a nuanced response based on a mix of immediate data, future projections, and the crucial variables of sentiment and global geopolitics. His brain combined the expert opinions, placing in a hierarchy the abstract considerations of diplomatic impact to the concrete steps of military action. Reviewing difficult decision-making, Brown University neuroscientist Michael Frank studied exactly how expert decision-makers combine and

129

fuse mental models.

Frank examined the so-called mixture of strietal experts (MoSE), a blend of neural mechanisms emulating a mixture of experts (MoE) in machine learning, to explain the human brain at peak performance. Unexpectedly, biologically inspired AI might reveal the brain's capabilities and close the gap between the two. In particular, Frank details how this advanced ML method to combine models has convergent design with prefrontal cortex mechanisms.[59] MoE has been cited as instrumental to OpenAI's generative AI performance.[60] Frank's research describes the computational model for how our brains manage to process and apply abstract rules rapidly, especially in complex, hierarchical environments.

By parceling the prefrontal cortex, the part responsible for higher cognitive functions like decision-making and planning, Frank maps cortex hierarchy, where the anterior (forward) parts handle more abstract representations. According to the proposed model, different parts of the cortex work together with another brain region called the striatum and the pleasure neurotransmitter dopamine. The striatum helps in gating (controlling) the input and output of information to the cortex and also plays a key role in influencing our responses. Dopamine facilitates learning at all levels of this brain circuit by signaling reward prediction errors – how the actual reward contrasts with what was expected.

The model suggests that this system enables "if-then" hypothesis testing, and thus, it learns rapidly in environments with a hierarchical structure. He connects the biology to a Bayesian RL mechanism that estimates the most likely mental state of a participant based on their observed sequence of decisions and rewards. The study corroborates theory with functional MRI (fMRI) studies. By visualizing blood oxygenation in the brain, fMRI reveals which parts of the brain turn on. On a conceptual mapping task, fMRI recordings indicate that when people learn new rules, multiple levels of abstraction are processed simultaneously, and the anterior parts of the cortex are activated for more abstract rules. On a conceptual mapping task, fMRI recordings indicate when people learn new rules, when multiple levels of abstraction process simultaneously, and when the anterior cortex activates for more abstract rules.

By combining insights with the ML computational model, Frank explains neural mechanisms supporting abstract rule discovery and the hierarchical structure of cognitive control in the human brain. Continuing his series in the journal Cerebral Cortex, Frank suggests that learning at different levels of the hierarchy can be guided by a single reward prediction error signal.[61] This signal is modulated by the attentional weight, or the degree to which a rule at a particular level contributed to a response. They propose that this signal is communicated to all parts of the cortical network, but its impact on neural activity depends on the strength of locks in a cascade. This supports a gated frontal cortex hypothesis of executive function.

In simple terms, Frank's work suggests using a Bayesian MoE system allows humans to learn and adapt to complex situations effectively. The front-most regions of the cortex manage more abstract information, while other areas handle more concrete data. The division of labor allows us to create and test hypotheses quickly, helping us navigate and learn in environments with complex, layered structures like Kennedy's dilemma. In our testing, MoE AI often charts the middle way, controlling risk to balance relevant factors.

Among ML scientists, the debate between biological inspiration is an ongoing debate, with some claiming no relation and others like Frank, using advances in both fields for cross-fertilization. The truth is likely more subtle – that there are undiscovered rules which, which in the analogy of powered flight

131

compared with biological flight, will reveal both approaches' true capability. As these two disciplines intertwine, we move closer to creating financial AI that is as agile and adaptive as the human mind.

7.1 Dopamine – Analogs in Neural Networks

We introduced the neurotransmitter dopamine as the brain's pleasure signal. The mechanism of dopamine is profound, connecting to the tech that elevates LLMs to generative AI. Scientists have long thought of dopamine as a sort of learning stamp, reinforcing connections between situations, actions, and rewards in our brain. This recalls RL in AI, where a reward is given for an action.

Recent research from Google Deepmind describes a deeper explanation.[62] This new perspective says dopamine is training the cortex to be its own standalone learning system. In other words, rather than merely reinforcing connections, dopamine might be helping the cortex learn how to learn. The cortex is shown to carry out tasks that look a lot like RL. But the relationship between these two systems, dopamine-based RL and the cortex's own RL, has been unclear. While dopamine helps adjust the learning system of the prefrontal cortex through its traditional RL role, this process ends up creating a second, more efficient learning algorithm within the cortex itself. This new learning algorithm in the cortex is suited to the task environment, can balance exploration and exploitation, and progressively adjusts its action policy.

The brain's dopamine system is teaching the cortex to be a better learner. The cortex doesn't mimic the learning history of dopamine, rather creates a more sophisticated one suited to the task at hand. Furthermore, the meta-learning RL model emulates the role of the cortex in integrating actions and rewards as an evolving representation of value, thus presenting an alternative understanding of how the cortex functions. The model's performance is consistent with observations of neuronal activity in the cortex.

The meta-RL framework resolves puzzling findings related to the roles of dopamine and cortex. It provides new insights into reward-based learning and generates testable predictions. For instance, it suggests that cortex's role in model-based control results from dopamine-driven synaptic learning. Further, the theory predicts that disruption to periodic dopamine signaling during initial training could impair the emergence of model-based control. The researchers sought to elucidate the cause and effect for model-based control.

Researchers introduced a new benchmark task called Alchemy.[63] Where traditional RL systems have a single task, meta-learning requires a whole range of tasks sharing some structure. Their system learns faster with each new task it encounters. As the game progresses, the system must learn and adapt to changes to perform well, making it an ideal test for meta-learning capabilities. In the ever dynamic market environment, durable performance requires meta-learning to improve processes. On the financial statements, value investors might infer meta-learning progress when they encounter gross or operating margin expansion. Meta-learning or learning to improve is a topic that has long fascinated investors including Munger's favored Founding Father, Benjamin Franklin. Unsurprisingly, it is a hallmark of effective business management.

Sliding Window vs. Forward Chaining cross validation

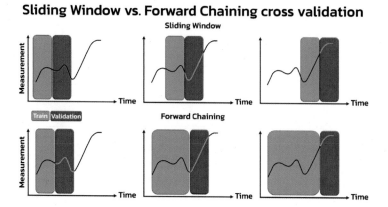

Figure 7.1: Forward chaining progressively grows the training set while using a held-out in time test set.

7.2 Combining Time Series Data with Natural Language

We examined how biological inspiration is improving causal AI. Unexpectedly, directly using causality in the TVTP (sec. 2.1) is effective. Forward chaining, also known as forward reasoning or walk-forward validation, bakes in causality inherent in the time series setting. The idea is to make the training set grow over time while keeping the test set as a fixed size window that moves forward in time (fig. 7.1). This method respects the temporal order of the data.

Importantly, forward chaining window size hedges survivorship bias, that the dataset is overly optimistic, in two ways. The writer Hemingway observed bankruptcy occurs, "gradually, and then suddenly". Unusually, tightening the resolution of the chaining window hones in on gradual decline, converging onto the solution from indices. Indices that focus on the top 1000 companies proactively remove companies in decline. By keeping pace with index cleaning, survivorship bias is mitigated. Forward chaining thus aligns well with a bottom-up approach to reasoning, where the starting point is available data, and logical conclusions or predictions are made based on this data. It's particularly useful in situations where the initial data is well-understood, such as a recent period of valuations, and the objective is to forecast near-term effects.

For causal modeling, forward chaining promotes correct learning. Causal modeling prefers cause-and-effect relationships. Forward chaining naturally integrates with this framework using a starting scenario, and permitting cause-and-effect relationships. As the chaining process progresses, it moves in the direction of these causal links, making it an intuitive and effective way to transition from cause to effect.

NLU can be effectively integrated with economic indicators for multi-modal analysis. A typical macro approach encompasses more than 35 types of economic indicators, including metrics like the Federal Funds Rate, Consumer Price Index, and Unemployment Rate, among others. The goal is to offer a practical, task-oriented perspective on economic trends that are inherently time-sensitive and operate on different time scales. We indicate the symbol used with the Federal Reserve Economic Database (FRED).

The Federal Funds Rate (FEDFUNDS) is the interest rate at which depository institutions lend reserve balances to other depository institutions overnight. It's set by the Federal Reserve and serves as a benchmark for other interest rates in the economy. In contrast, the Repo Rate (SOFR) or Secured Overnight Financing Rate, is the cost of borrowing cash overnight collateralized by Treasury securities. SOFR more accurately reflects the cost of short-term borrowing to companies.

The M2 Money Stock (M2) comprises cash, checking deposits,

and easily convertible near-money. It's a broad measure of a nation's money supply and is used to understand the availability of liquidity in the economy. The Consumer Price Index (CPI-AUCSL) measures the average change in the prices for a market basket of consumer goods and services to probe inflation.

The Unemployment Rate (UNRATE) measures the percentage of the total labor force that is unemployed but actively seeking employment. It's a key indicator of labor market conditions. The Industrial Production Index (INDPRO) measures the real output of all relevant establishments located in the US, regardless of their ownership, but not those located in US territories. It's often used as a barometer for the overall health of the industrial sector. Real Gross Domestic Product (GDPC1) measures the value of all finished goods and services produced, adjusted for changes in price or inflation. The Personal Savings Rate (PSAVERT) is the ratio of personal income saved to personal net disposable income.

The Consumer Confidence Index (UMCSENT) taps into the financial pulse of households across the country, measuring whether people are optimistic or pessimistic about economic prospects. If consumers are feeling good, they spend more, and that lifts the economy. Producer Price Index for All Commodities (PPI-ACO) plays a similar role, albeit from the other side of the aisle. It monitors how much domestic producers are charging for their goods. It's a handy crystal ball for predicting consumer inflation down the line.

When it comes to the property market, Housing Starts (HOUST) is the yardstick. It tracks the number of new homes under construction each month, signaling the health of the residential construction sector. The more new builds, the more optimistic developers are about future demand.

Real Disposable Personal Income (DSPIC96) uncovers what's left in household coffers after the taxman has had his share.

Meanwhile, Retail Sales Total Excluding Food Services (RSXFS) paints a vivid picture of consumer spending behavior, tallying up how much stores are selling each month.

On the business side, a key barometer is Business Inventories (BUSINV). This metric tells you how much stock is sitting in the warehouses of manufacturers, wholesalers, and retailers. If these numbers shift suddenly, it's a hint that costly inventory is dragging on a sluggish economy.

Wage growth is captured by Average Hourly Earnings of All Employees, Total Private (CES0500000003). This indicator serves as a spotlight on income trends in the private sector, often tipping us off about inflationary pressures. Manufacturing Sector Real Output (OUTMS) adds another layer, revealing the real-world value of goods churned out by factories, adjusted for inflation.

The auto industry's health is laid bare by Total Vehicle Sales (TOTALSA), while the Import Price Index All Commodities (IR) and Export Price Index All Commodities (IX) serve as gatekeepers for trade balance. Capacity Utilization Total Industry (TCU) completes the industrial picture by indicating how efficiently we're using our production capabilities.

The employment scenario isn't just numbers – it's people and families. Non-Farm Payroll (PAYEMS) unveils the job landscape, excluding certain sectors like farming and private households. Fluctuations in this metric make or break political careers. Another politically sensitive item on the energy economy is captured by Crude Oil Prices West Texas Intermediate (WTISPLC) and the Gasoline and Diesel Fuel Update (GASREGW). These numbers tell us how much it costs to fuel our lives and can have ripple effects throughout the economy.

US Natural Gas Wellhead Price (MHPG) keeps tabs on natural gas prices, and Initial Claims (ICSA) are an early-warning system for layoffs. If more people are filing for unemployment, tough times could be ahead.

Several other indicators, from ISM Manufacturing PMI Composite Index (ISM) to US Treasury Budget, Total Receipts (MTSR) and Federal Surplus or Deficit (FYFSD), serve as the nuts and bolts holding the economic structure together. They help understand federal revenue streams and the government's fiscal health.

Chicago Fed National Activity Index (CFNAI) and the Advance Monthly Sales reports (MARTS and RSAFS) round out the picture, providing invaluable insights into overall economic activity and sales trends in retail and food services.

The next time the state of the economy is baffling, these are the breadcrumbs. They can help navigate through a shifting environment, bringing a complex picture into sharper focus. When incorporating macroeconomic data into an AI model, it's crucial to normalize the data effectively. Models perform better when input data has zero mean and unit variance, or is at least similarly scaled. The architecture of the model should be aptly chosen. For instance, a multi-input model should separately process company-specific and macroeconomic data before combining them, allowing the model to better learn from each data type.

7.3 Finance and Meta-language

Language philosopher Wittgenstein remarked, "the word 'this' has been called the only genuine name; so that anything else we call a name was one only in an inexact, approximate sense." It's natural that language is an important tool to enhance financial statements, which describe businesses. Financial statements, while powerfully condensing business performance for comparison, come at a cost. As we discussed, the curse of shadows is the age-old trap related in Plato's "The Republic". When confined to an abstracted description, agents can fathom shadows on a cave wall as indicative of true forces at play. Language is an effective method by which finance aspires to escape the curse of shadows.

We had mentioned jargon as a veil on business fundamentals. In order to get up to speed, an authority such as the venture firm Andreessen Horowitz (A16Z) has tasked its managers to become developers. In 2023, a partner at A16Z sheepishly admitted their server for an AI model went offline due to budget triggers.[64] Unsurprisingly, venture partners don't become AI developers overnight. As Stanford lecturer Peter Mohanty wryly critiqued the film Armageddon, "it's easier for an astronaut to become a miner, than the other way around". Yet the roughneck miners have the greatest heart, and crossing the chasm is the right instinct.

Wittgenstein mentioned language as recursive and adjacent, like a fractal. He could've been describing the formless form of generative AI training. Unlike most of AI and ML work, generative AI doesn't limit itself to one task. It's trained like a sculpture hammered in from all sides to form the correct facets. The fractal nature gives infinite detail in the smallest region that can overwhelm the investor. Only when the fractal pattern can be appreciated, either through Buffett's exhaustive reading or language AI, is when value investing reaches its apex. At current levels, AI generates the form from which an investor can perceive deeper into the pattern.

7.4 Bootstrapping Ability

Laws of learning apply to both humans and machines. Early research suggests that humans and machines learn in similar ways, especially through curriculum learning. In curriculum learning, a machine starts by learning from simple examples, much like a beginner. The structure for curriculum learning is to show semantically accessible and distributionally relevant data sources.

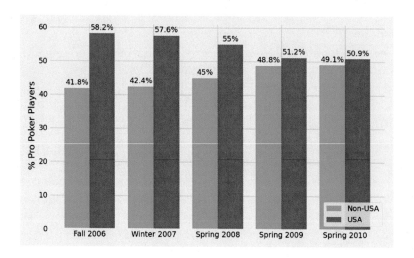

Figure 7.2: Non-US vs US top poker players[65]

For instance, when we worked on object detection we developed a procedure. First, mine easy images (low uncertainty) and use them to train the detector. Then, show images based on uncertainty while making sure the images match our distribution. Giving the right piece of the puzzle at the appropriate moment stimulates learning.

The way learning can go awry is as remarkably informative as when it goes right. Let's consider the example of my college roommate, an expert in poker. When I was in college pounding physics textbooks, Scott sat at our dorm desk furiously check raising on live money online poker. In 2006, the Unlawful Internet Gambling Enforcement Act (UIGEA) was passed, which made it illegal for financial institutions to process transactions related to online gambling, including online poker. This led to online poker sites ending operations in the US. Domestic online live money stakes evaporated in short order.

In our curriculum learning vocabulary, domain relevant training examples ceased. According to Statista, the number of top poker players from the US dropped from 58.2% in Fall 2006 to 50.9% in Spring 2010 (fig. 7.2). Paper accounts are never the same as live money stakes. The government had crippled poker learning, an externality to their regulation. Humans and machines need quality learning environments to reach their potential. Scott used online poker to build competency, and he went on to a successful career in Las Vegas. We discussed earlier how financial filing quality varies from the largest 1000 domestic companies compared to the next 7000 companies. Now, we intuit that the reason is fundamentally a data quality effect.

If we apply the moral of our story, investment managers that focus on product predictions should cut their teeth in actual business conditions. The meta-domain of financial analysis is part of the learning environment for reasoning. The Head of Sales usually gets the CEO nod over the CFO. Computational and physical sciences excel in their open disclosure and rich set of challenges to hone abilities. Similarly, pushing AI to prove theorems isn't an idle task. Like pushing a race car to new limits, it brings a host of associated benefits, not least of which is well-posed curriculum learning. According to industry insiders, the curriculum learning recipe powers GPT-4 over other generative AIs.

7.5 The Investment Development Cycle

In software engineering, the development cycle is well-understood. While Buffett and Munger have outlined the investment thesis development cycle, it has rarely been spelled out. When the process is laid out, generative AI is an accelerant to the investment development cycle. The head of private equity at Blackstone describes, "The starting point in the investment process is the creation of a first-task memo by junior staff. Nowadays, in most cases, writing a first-task memo still requires two or three days to dig through data, build analyses and models, and produce a detailed plan that is intelligible to Blackstone executives and limited partners."[66] A typical engineering cycle means gathering requirements, designing systems, implementation, and testing. Blackstone now uses AI to set the stage in hours instead of days. Then, like a value investor, Blackstone engages their critical thinking.

Generative AI can accelerate the conscious and subconscious maturation cycle. Often, an intellect like Buffett will devour an enormous amount of information. In Nvidia's approach, CEO Huang insisted on Sunday status reports, a deliberate habit as destiny to engage one more subconscious cycle. Over the courses of weeks, the conscious and subconscious synthesize the sum of the investor's experience to render an investing thesis.

For requirements gathering, this could be understanding the investor's goals, risk tolerance, constraints, and areas of interest. The AI can assist in this process by structuring the investor's portfolio and macro focus. System design for investments means identifying and structuring potential instruments. Implementation may fall on RL, as we discussed earlier, to execute trades. Finally, where quants have their historical back-testing, generative AI allows historical scenario testing. By identifying and playing forward various scenarios, two strengths are collected. Generative AI serves as a plausibility filter, reflecting human patterns. Second, LLMs have in-grained causality through the mechanism of causal language modeling and as one of the key benchmarks in SuperGLUE evaluation. This causal insight gives value investors an edge over quants, who often get lost in complex calculations.

The investment development cycle is primarily creative. Carnegie Mellon University Professor Po-Shen Loh spends much of his time with the US National Mathematics team teaching them how to approach problems that they've never seen before. Advanced mathematics is inherently creative. Loh spends his time inventing new frameworks and applying them. He finds enormous potential in using generative AI for his work.[67] The creative cycle concludes when causal mechanisms are identified, completing the investment development cycle.

8 Portfolio Optimization: Balancing Risk and Return with ML

Victor Haghani, a founding partner at the ill-fated LTCM, lost over \$100M personally when he failed to balance risk and return.[68] Was he not aware of basic risk management through CAPM? CAPM has been a cornerstone in the field of financial management for its straightforward approach to balancing risk and return in a portfolio. Yet Buffett's two-part risk approach trumps CAPM for intelligent investing. Buffett's approach balances risk and return by respecting, "risk comes from not knowing what you're doing" and "diversification is a protection against ignorance. It makes very little sense for those who know what they're doing." Remarkably, an AI approach can be designed for Buffett's criteria.

Consider managing a portfolio with three asset classes of government bonds, blue-chip stocks, and high-volatility tech stocks. Each of these assets have varying degrees of risk and return. CAPM offers a crutch for investors who don't delve into the details. Such investors know government bonds are generally low-risk with lower returns, akin to a savings account. Blue-chip stocks offer moderate risk and moderate returns. High-volatility tech stocks are risky and offer high returns. Their goal in portfolio management is to find the weights without developing fundamental understanding. Simpler models like CAPM remain prevalent because of their ease of use. Yet, as computational power and AI techniques advance, accurate intelligence is increasingly achievable, offering Buffett's sophisticated value approach to balancing risk and return.

The challenge lies not just in gauging the individual risk and return characteristics of each asset, but also in understanding how they interact with each other. The financial landscape is influenced by multiple variables like market conditions, interest rates, and geopolitical events, among others. Incorporating these factors makes the portfolio generation far more complex. For example, you'll need to consider not just the performance of individual assets, but also how they are affected by economic cycles, the health of the sectors they belong to, and global events. To control the first category of Buffett risk, AI ratings limit the errors of omission by comprehensively surveilling the investment landscape. For the second category, AI corroborates findings to build conviction for concentrated investment for significant returns.

This is how ML and AI techniques are useful. We'll discuss confidence-based approaches, Bayesian approaches that incorporate human judgement, and structurally hedged portfolio construction. Allocations are built by sifting through large datasets, identifying patterns, and adapting to new data, providing a nuanced understanding of asset behavior and interdependencies.

8.1 Active Portfolio Management: Confidence

Active quantitative management adds a confidence level to expected returns to propagate risk robustly. Buffett's punch card example indicates exactly how much confidence is needed in value investing. Buffett proposes that you have a punch card indicating twenty investments for your lifetime. Then each selection must be made with the most comprehensive care. The general idea is the more confident in one of the selections, the more capital the investor would allocate. Short-term investments, which are based on statistical and market making tactics, take many small bets like the house edge for a casino. Given that RenTech has topped out at \$500M AUM, Buffett's method is different than market making – there just isn't enough scale there. RenTech, in launching a value fund, embarked on something far afield from their core competency. Value investors incorporate the confidence level because the best outcome is to make few investments with high confidence.

An intuitive feel for confidence level is observed every day. When the meteorologist says there's a 70% chance of rainy weather, do you bring your umbrella? While at the famed Bell Labs, the physicist John Kelly approached confidence factors in a seminal work.[23] Kelly used the analogy of a confidence (probability) that equates to some practical level of correctness (error rate) of a source. Kelly determined the recommended allocation even in the presence of errors to grow the asset value as quickly as possible. Critics argue that the method's recommended allocations are highly sensitive to minor variations in the error rate. While one solace is that where many quant models swing wildly with hand-picked parameters, AI models provide a first-principles estimate of confidence levels on a relative value basis. We had mentioned the anecdote of the Deepmind researcher who in an earlier life found the absurd practice of selecting an arbitrary volatility value. AI confidence with Kelly's criterion equates at least to an axiomatically tight framework within intrinsic relative value. AI confidence at least gives a good intra-asset equity valuation model for the investor.

In keeping with Buffett's investing as a business framework, executives and investors must bear the task of integration models at the highest levels of responsibility. Extending this idea, futurist Cixin Liu conceptualized Wall Facers, individuals prepared to counter pervasive espionage threats. In his imagining, a Wall Facer alone holds a master plan of his own design. His concept engages with the American concept of the executive, the prime example of Truman's desk sign, "The Buck Stops Here". A Wall Facer's job is to not reveal the entire plan for reasons of defense, instead issuing directives to gradually assemble the big picture. In a landscape rife with industrial espionage, the Wall Facer paradigm is often still in effect for many executives, and the financial filings are only a hint of the master plan. A Fischer-style detective approach is needed. AI approaches add comprehensive analysis to piece together the puzzle.

8.2 The 130/30 Fund Structure

Like CAPM, hedging is structural concept meant to contain risk and promote reward. Unlike CAPM, the long borrow structure is almost an imperative for active managers, and startlingly missed with most mutual funds and ETFs. To contemplate its effects, take a straight-forward projection of assets given a compounding rate. In a rule of thumb dating back at least 100 years, all investment compounders are subject to the rule of 72. The rule of 72 goes like this – take your return rate, for example 8% yearly return on a diversified market portfolio is reasonable. Divide 72 by the 8% rate, to yield 9 years. It'll take 9 years to double an investment at the 8% rate. In the opening figure of Chapter 1, we took a conservative 7% as the base rate.

For a universal method to increase the rate of return, a simplistic answer is to leverage, that is accept a higher level of risk return via financial arrangement. Leverage is the siren's call to any financial operation, full of allure and danger. There are at least three ways of leverage available to common investors. (1) We can borrow money, either through a loan at a bank or revolving credit, (2) we can engage in derivatives which are complex financial instruments, or (3) we can borrow securities against so-called marginable securities as an asset-backed loan and immediately lend them out to another investor, the complex arrangement known simply as short-selling (borrowing and immediate lending).

The most common hedged structure, the 130/30 long short portfolio has a long history. Carol Loomis writing for Fortune magazine in 1966 ascribed the technique to Alfred Jones, a PhD sociologist.[69] Buffett goes on to contradict Loomis, ascribing securities borrowing to his mentor Graham in the Thirties. Buffett himself approached commercial banks early on to borrow securities. Allegedly, the story went that they asked him which stocks he wanted to borrow. He answered, "why any that you would be willing to lend me", which deepens the present riddle. Why is the 130/30 long borrow posture structurally sound?

As Jones originally called it, "speculative techniques for conservative ends", the hedged nature is key. 130/30 uses leverage specifically in a hedged posture. When borrowing 30% of securities to buy 30% more securities, the expected equity exposure would be an additional 60% from 30+30 (a nominal 160% gross exposure). Instead, the exposure is more nearly 0%, meaning net exposure of 100%. The reason being the short 30% and the long 30% are hedged, meaning their market risk mostly offsets each other. Thereby we expect in excess of the market return while exposing only to the base unity amount of risk. This is why Buffett was willing to short even a presumably random sample of securities.

Leverage is more safely employed when it's structurally hedged. The next piece is that the cost of borrowing securities is exceptionally low, leading to an economical cost of capital. Known as the borrow rate, for liquid large companies, the rate is usually on the order of 25 basis points plus the dividend yield. The borrow rate is a floating rate that fluctuates with supply and demand.

If there are fewer owners of the security willing to lend it out, the owners are able to charge a higher price. Because of elastic supply and demand relation, borrowing securities should be performed carefully, namely always with stop loss limits determined in advance of entering and revisable only to tighter limits. Further, triggering stop loss on the borrow side must translate to a bracket on the long side to rein in the leveraged exposure. Another point is that by borrowing the security and lending it out, you are on the hook for the dividends paid out by the security too. Nonetheless, such provision is vastly superior than the margin rate on cash, which when the Federal Reserve increases the Fed Funds Rate, can easily exceed 5%.

So once the 130/30 structure is in place, we can use the framework of alpha, the active management contribution to return. If a manager is able to deliver 1% of alpha on a portfolio, our previous example would net 8% + 1% equaling 9% of total return. With the 130/30 exposure in place, now the return could rough out to 160% of alpha, meaning 1.6%. If we use the rule of 72, we expect doubling our investment every 7.5 years instead of 9 years. We've saved 1.5 years of time in the compounding world at a better risk tradeoff than margining cash.

There are some caveats to mention with an abundance of caution. Buffett and Munger mention at least one regarding promoters who would pump up the price of a security for no reason connected to intrinsic value, no doubt an occurrence as common as financial bubbles. This is a practical concern and constrains the concentration of borrowed positions. Even more drastic, there's the discrete nature of markets that can gap prices, say via private market acquisitions, taking private, or long-tailed behavior. Yet more reasons to preclude concentration. Already one solution comes to us from Buffett. By borrowing against a diversified basket of securities, a market ETF, we can eliminate some of the granular borrow side risk at the cost of the alpha on the borrow side. Perhaps a small price to pay to bend the arc of time safely.

Then there's the question of why not a higher ratio, say 140/40 or 150/50. The level has to do with the lending requirements on net asset value (NAV). Holding to 30% borrow against NAV means the account will be far away from a margin call. Generally only if the marketable value of the long positions fell by 70% would the account expect a margin call. Domestically, there is only one occurrence of this over a multiyear period. During the Wall Street Crash of 1929, the Dow fell about 89% from its peak in 1929 to its low in 1932, and maximally about 52.7% in 1931.

Now circling around, there's another reason not to use leverage. If there's no expected alpha, then there's no point in the long borrow posture. The simple example is borrowing a whole market basket to buy a whole market basket is the equivalent of 1 plus -1 equals 0, and in this case a little worse since there's the borrow cost and transaction fees. In value investing, we expect a positive alpha, but it's far from guaranteed. The founder of Vanguard, John Bogle likes to point out that 90% of active investors underperform the market.[26]

Finally, not all brokers allow borrowing securities. Even more sadistic, some brokers promote leverage via options, with cost of capital easily ranging above 30% (yes greater than 30 times our 1%), not to mention brokers selling order flow, stacking the deck against you. Note, if you do insist on derivatives, adjust the NAV accordingly after closing positions.

Now a few loose ends. According to Buffett and Munger, Buffett doesn't use the 130/30 structure anymore. Some of the reason is once in the upper echelons of capitalism, it's not exactly sporting to borrow huge chunks of other companies stock. Famously, Elon Musk refused to contribute to Bill Gates' environmental efforts due to his open short on Tesla.[70;71] There's other elements that limit large capacity centered around market impact when choosing borrow targets, related to trade execution (sec. 3.6).

With that, we convey an overview of the mechanistic strength of a 130/30 portfolio structure. It's structurally hedged, has a low cost of capital, and is readily accessible to most investors. It does mean additional complexity, and the fact remains 90% of active managers underperform the market. Leverage never helps the underperforming manager and causes the red marks on hedge fund performance that Buffett points out. Now that we have CAPM and 130/30 in our toolbox, how does ML fit in, and what would the discipline of intrinsic investing have to contribute?

8.3 Opposing Forces: Stability Through Tension

When we described Buffett's risk framework, Kelly confidence sizing, and 130/30 structure, opposing forces are the unifying principle. Stability through tension gives resiliency with an ultimate connection to the core of intrinsic value investing. Opposing forces pervade nature and society for good reason.

Tempered glass induces compressive stress on the interior plane and tensile stress on the exterior. These opposing forces create the material's increased strength and shatter-resistance. Pre-stressed concrete employs a similar principle – steel cables under tension are embedded within concrete under compression. This interplay between tension and compression makes the material more resilient against external forces, enhancing its structural integrity. In biological systems, bones and muscles work in tandem where bones are responsible for compressive strength and muscles offer tensile strength. This dynamism allows for both rigidity and flexibility in skeletons, enhancing mobility and support.

In society, the Founding Fathers used checks and balances to create a resilient structure keeping any group from gaining excessive power. In electrical circuits, inductors and capacitors balance opposing forces through storage and release, resistance and yielding. From Maxwell's equations, inductors store energy in the magnetic potential when electrical current passes through them, while capacitors store energy via the electric field. This balance regulates energy flow, making electrical grids adaptable and resilient.

Intrinsic value investors align like owner operators, while using the opposing force of dispassionate distance for reserved counsel. Operational management develop products with a go-to market mission. They control for risk in the business and product, hedging out operational concerns only in as so much to smooth operations. For instance, Southwest Airlines counters broad global stimulus by hedging out rising fuel costs with futures contracts. [72] Where operational management has a narrow view, investment management shoulders the burden for comprehensive information. This explains Buffett and Munger's success as central relays for their sprawling network of businesses. Media companies, such as Capital Cities and CEO Tom Murphy, used this format effectively. Further, LLM methods, as a comprehensive intellect, serve value investors in the exhaustive and endless evaluation of business conditions.

9 Pathways to Performance: Metrics, and Insights

It wasn't going fast enough for Jeff Dean, the manager of Google's AI division. He wanted to accelerate AI development on his teams. Dean knew that tightly coupling development with feedback for the engineer was paramount for time to solution. He drew on his own inspirations as one of the top technical architects of Google's search engine infrastructure. For his contributions, Google engineers had immortalized him with Jeff Dean memes that riffed on Chuck Norris jokes. One went, "the compiler (an automated code system) doesn't warn Jeff, he warns the compiler." Dean, who had taken leadership of Google Brain, knew that ML experiments, if unmonitored, could balloon in time, with one early ML experiment allegedly running nine months on their first generation DistBelief framework. Dean's solution used a directed acyclic graph (DAG), a computation diagram that flowed like a river, and most importantly allowed interaction in the computation process, much like substations along a river. The DAG approach was proved out with the efficient vision network InceptionV3, which used three sampling points (loss monitors), and won second place in the 2015 ImageNet competition. Dean understood the developer, in charge of creating new paradigms, needed a flexible way of meta-learning or designing his feedback environment. We explore how learning and meta-learning is core to value investing and AI progress, especially generative AI.

In ML, so-called self-supervision enforces consistency in a common sense way. Self-consistency is prized socially, especially by millennials. Millennials abhor hypocrisy, violation of consistency in beliefs. The millennial generation has been criticized for demanding consistency. One weakness in self-consistency and perhaps the critique from older generations is that self-consistency penalizes ambiguity, any one to many mapping. Meanwhile, base translation systems use the self-supervised cycle consistency method since meaning should be preserved. Cycle consistency would translate a passage from English to French and then back to English again. In investing, we can practice self-supervision via retrospective analysis, which puts us in the shoes of professional evaluators. The emerging CAIA certificant is an analyst meant to conduct due diligence for pension funds and institutions, and their evaluations are a reasonable viewpoint. They outline a few concerns – filtering the closet indexer and the non-scaler, detected by comparing time weighted versus dollar weighted returns.

A closet indexer is an actively managed fund that claims to generate alpha (i.e., above-market returns) but in reality closely mirrors the performance of a benchmark index. Essentially, the fund is charging higher fees for active management while delivering performance that could be achieved with a cheaper index fund. By comparing the time-weighted and dollar-weighted returns of a fund to those of a benchmark index, one can determine how closely the fund's performance aligns with the index. If the returns are very similar, the fund might be a closet indexer. The time-weighted return removes the effect of cash flows into and out of the fund, focusing solely on the fund's investment performance. The dollar-weighted return, on the other hand, accounts for the timing and amount of investor cash flows, providing a measure of the actual investor experience.

A non-scaler is an investment fund or strategy that performs well with a small amount of assets but faces difficulties when trying to scale up its operations. This could be due to various factors, such as liquidity constraints or market impact costs, which become more significant as the fund grows in size. Here, the comparison between time-weighted and dollar-weighted returns could reveal a non-scaler by showing that the investment strategy does not hold up well when more capital is involved. A consistent divergence between these two types of returns could be a red flag. For instance, if the time-weighted return looks promising but the dollar-weighted return is lagging, it could indicate that the strategy doesn't scale effectively with increasing assets. Examining order sizes versus average trading volume can prospectively identify non-scaling.

Unsurprisingly, internal metrics have far-reaching consequences in ML and management. We now discuss the strong influence ML objectives have on performance.

9.1 ML Objective Functions: Function and Purpose

Objective functions in ML are called loss functions because they focus on errors to drive corrections to the neural network. ML loss functions (fig. 9.1) sit atop performance metrics in portfolio management since their aim is learning. Like Buffett planning for the long-term, NNs target improvement in a myriad of ways. In the context of linear fit, the mean squared error (MSE) pioneered by Gauss is similar to the concept of tracking error in portfolio management. Just as the tracking error measures the standard deviation of the difference between a portfolio's returns and its benchmark's returns, MSE calculates the average of the squares of the errors between the predicted and actual values. It's sensitive to large errors, much like how tracking errors can be significantly impacted by large discrepancies between a portfolio and its benchmark. MSE enforces fidelity to a degree that's

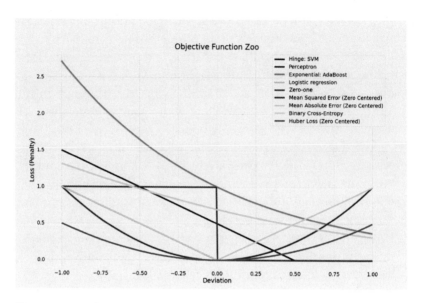

Figure 9.1: Objective functions like performance metrics reflect a function and purpose

too punitive for early stages in learning.

Mean absolute error (MAE) is similar to absolute drawdown in a portfolio, which measures the absolute loss from peak to trough. MAE is less sensitive to extreme values, making it more robust when there are outliers or when the data is skewed. It focuses on the magnitude of errors without overly penalizing large errors, similar to how absolute drawdown considers the magnitude of losses but does not square them.

Huber loss can be seen as a hybrid of tracking error and absolute drawdown. It works like MSE for small errors and like MAE for large errors. Imagine a portfolio evaluation metric that uses tracking error for returns within a certain range but switches to absolute drawdown when returns diverge significantly from the benchmark. This would be more forgiving of extreme events, similar to how Huber Loss is more robust to outliers.

In classification problems, binary cross-entropy or log loss is comparable to the Sharpe ratio, which gauges risk-adjusted returns. Just as the Sharpe ratio evaluates the performance of an investment by adjusting for its risk, log loss measures the performance of a binary classification model by taking into account the predicted probabilities. It provides a more nuanced view than just counting misclassifications, making it useful for probabilistic predictions.

For multi-class classification problems, categorical cross-entropy is used. It extends the concept of Binary cross-entropy to multiple classes, much like how a multi-asset portfolio evaluation would extend the Sharpe ratio calculations to account for multiple asset classes.

Hinge loss can be related to the concept of a MoS in value investing. The loss function aims to not just correctly classify, but also maximize the margin between classes, ensuring a buffer like how we look for a high intrinsic value than price to minimize downside risk. The hinge loss, with its flat region, mimics Buffett's propensity for inaction. In the flat region, no change is sent.

In specialized scenarios, Kullback-Leibler (KL) Divergence serves a prized role that would resonate with Buffett's love of non-transitive dice, the didactic distributions toy.[73] The KL divergence quantifies the difference between two probability distributions by calculating how much one diverges from the other. In this sense, it's akin to a sophisticated risk assessment tool that doesn't just look at a single metric, but evaluates the entire distribution of returns or outcomes. In investment management, imagine if you had a complex model of the expected returns of an asset, taking into account various scenarios, economic conditions, and other variables, resulting in a probability distribution of expected returns. This could compare to the actual distribution of returns based on historical data. The KL Divergence allows an integrative comparison between two distributions in a comprehensive manner.

Cosine similarity and intersection over union (IoU) are more specialized loss functions. Cosine Similarity can be likened to correlation coefficients between asset returns in a portfolio, while IoU is more like measuring the overlap between targeted and actual portfolio holdings. IoU is particularly useful in imaging applications, like segmenting tumors or identifying pedestrians.

Loss functions in ML serve as the guiding metrics for model training, much like how various performance and risk metrics guide investment decisions. Choosing the right loss function is selecting the right evaluation metric for an investment strategy, as both set the course for optimization efforts. Grove famously chided Christensen for not taking this to heart. AI engineers mix and match the concepts, and even tailor bespoke ones, much like a financial planner tailors for a client. For both roles, it's a justified and renewable fount of industry.

9.2 Forward testing

The forward test refers to live trading, the track record, or the out of sample test. We've examined the issue of the importance of forward testing from several angles already. When we examined ML competitions, the phenomenon of leaderboard shuffling shows exactly how principled the teams have been in their ML pipeline. Have they not fooled themselves by p-hacking their way to a high score on the validation set? The forward test is the investing world's impenetrable test dataset. For that reason it forms an invaluable check, but as Buffett might echo, it can't replace critical evaluation.

Forward testing is the perfectly enforced one shot TVTP. When we discussed track record, statistical analyses show why the track record must only remain a check. To recap, a good forward test would take too long (the best period is a lifetime) to be conclusive. When measuring a lifetime, managers age and change cognitive abilities. The case is the same for AI agents unless performance regressions are stringently measured.

The forward test for AI agents detects performance regression. A little dirty secret in technology and engineering divisions is that regressions happen all the time. It's what you do about it that matters. Without descending into minutiae (technical debt related to dependencies, bit rot, or personnel), engineers have well-studied frameworks and tools to address performance regressions. First, the mainstay is the shadow deployment. Two versions of the agent are deployed side-by-side with preferably the new agent in a sandbox environment. When the internal team or even white hat team is satisfied, the agent is moved to A/B testing, where segments of the world are shown one agent versus the other. From there, tradeoffs and differences are evaluated. The infrastructure for agile change is the institutional advantage that accrues to principled technology companies. A seamless engineering infrastructure builds on an abstracted computational layer, made increasingly accessible by cloud computing.

9.3 Model ensembling

We pick up the executive function we alluded to earlier, combining viewpoints. Model ensembling is the technique where multiple models are trained to solve the same problem and their predictions combined to produce the final prediction. Different models may capture different aspects of the data, and combining them can yield a more robust and accurate prediction. Whether confidence or accuracy determines model mixtures, the result is almost always beneficial over single models. Different models have varying strengths and weaknesses, and often it's straight-forward to determine the data space where a model is most effective.

Ensembling helps to average out the errors and reduce the variance in the predictions. This leads to more stable and reliable outcomes, which is especially beneficial when dealing with noisy data or models that are prone to overfitting (every problem is a nail, when your model's a hammer).

Ensembles also help in overcoming model limitations. No single model is perfect. Each has its own set of assumptions and limitations. However, an ensemble mitigates these issues by combining models that have complementary strengths. For example, one model might struggle with a particular feature, while another excels at it. When we discuss many-fold ensembling, we deliberately draw out this tendency through randomization.

Empirical evidence supports the efficacy of ensembling. In ML competitions, winning solutions almost always utilize ensemble methods. However, it's essential to note that ensembling comes with tradeoffs, including increased model complexity, computational costs, and potentially decreased interpretability.

Let's consider a hypothetical example where we have three different models used for predicting whether a particular stock's price will go up or down in the next trading day. Each of these models uses a different approach.

Buffett's investing originally followed the Grahamian model on book value and so-called "cigar butt" companies – those that may be out of favor but still have intrinsic value. The Buffett Model prioritizes fundamental analysis, examining a company's financial health, earnings, and market conditions before making an investment. With a keen eye for undervalued assets, the model has an accuracy rate of say 65% in generating positive returns. It's cautious, meticulous, and grounded in financial metrics, embodying Buffett's preference for businesses that are easy to understand and have a strong track record.

In contrast, Munger's investment approach could be represented by another model. This model is more adventurous, looking beyond traditional markets to places like China and focusing on growth potential and quality businesses. While it still uses fundamental analysis, it's also open to considering companies with higher valuations if they offer quality and growth. This model might have a slightly lower accuracy rate of 60%, but it aims for higher returns by investing in businesses with significant upside potential. Munger's philosophy is about finding quality businesses at fair prices, even if they aren't exactly bargains.

Suppose both the Buffett and Munger Models were used to make 100 investment predictions each. If their errors were uncorrelated – a key assumption – the ensemble of these two models could potentially offer an even higher rate of successful investments. Let's say the Buffett Model would make 65 correct predictions out of 100, and the Munger Model would make 60 correct predictions. By ensembling these models, one could take advantage of the conservative, value-driven approach of the Buffett Model while benefiting from the growth-oriented, quality-focused strategy of the Munger Model.

To estimate the combined accuracy of the Buffett and Munger Models, let's assume that their errors are independent. If the Buffett Model has an accuracy of 65% and the Munger Model has an accuracy of 60%, then when making 100 investment decisions, the Buffett Model would be expected to make 65 correct predictions, while the Munger Model would make 60. In a simplified scenario where the models' errors are uncorrelated, the ensemble approach would yield a correct prediction as long as at least one of the models is correct.

To estimate the ensemble's accuracy, one would need to consider the probabilities of both models being wrong simultaneously. If the Buffett Model has a 35% chance of being wrong and the Munger Model has a 40% chance of being wrong, the probability of both being wrong at the same time would be 14%. This means there's an 86% chance that at least one of the models would make a correct prediction. This would be a significant improvement, beyond double, over using either model individually, highlighting the power of ensemble methods in investment strategies.

Remember, these results will depend heavily on the specific characteristics of the models and the data. If the models' errors are highly correlated, ensembling may not provide a significant benefit. It's also important to ensure that the models are diverse and not just variations of the same underlying model. Even with relatively low-accuracy models, as long as their errors are uncorrelated, ensembling can provide a significant boost in predictive power. In the realm of securities analysis, this can translate to more accurate predictions and better investment decisions.

The idea of ensembling can extend beyond just ML models. It also applies to teams of humans and models working together. Let's consider an investment committee at a financial firm. Just as with the models, when individuals work together as a committee, their collective decision, arrived at through discussion and voting, is likely to be more accurate than most (or all) individual decisions. This is because each individual brings a unique perspective, helping to avoid the blind spots that might exist in a single person's or model's analysis. The diversity of opinions and approaches can mitigate the impact of any one person's biases or errors, leading to more robust decision-making. High performance leaders like Huang use this technique regularly.

Now, let's add our ensemble model to the committee. The model serves as a twelfth member, providing an additional perspective that's based on a different kind of analysis. The other committee members consider the model's prediction in their discussions and use it to challenge or support their own views.

In this setup, the humans and the model are working together in what's known as a hybrid or human-in-the-loop ensemble. The model's prediction can help the humans avoid cognitive biases or overlook important information, while the humans can bring their intuition, judgment, and ability to consider context into the mix. This setup takes advantage of the strengths of both humans and models, potentially leading to even better decisions. It elevates the primacy of diversity in decision-making – whether that diversity comes from different types of models, different people, or a mix of humans and machines.

9.4 Many-fold ensembling

We've already discussed how ensembling combines multiple models for accurate decisions and early on how cross-validation helps understand model performance. We introduce many-fold ensembling, adding another level of performance, though like continuous compounding, encounters diminishing returns. Many-fold (or k-folds) ensembling, taking different dataset partitions as training input, can power ensembling at fixed data requirements. The idea is that instead of making one model from the entire dataset, you build several different models on different subsets of the data to then average their predictions. The model ensemble isn't affected by intra-dataset quirks or anomalies.

Let's use a business example to illustrate this. A financial analyst in a company wants to segment customers based on their purchasing behavior. Instead of building one model using all the data, they use k-folds ensembling. Just like cross-validation, the analyst divides the available customer data into five distinct groups (folds) ensuring that each fold represents a random subset of the customer base. The next step is to train multiple models. For each of the five folds, the analyst leaves out that specific fold and trains a model using the data from the remaining four folds.

This process is repeated five times, each time with a different fold being left out for training on the remaining groups.

After the models have been trained, the focus shifts to testing and evaluation. Each of the five models is assessed using the fold that was excluded during its training, the cross-validation step covered in Chapter 2. The final step is to ensemble the predictions. The outcomes from all five models are either averaged or weighted to produce a more robust customer analysis. The key advantage of k-folds ensembling method is it incorporates multiple viewpoints from windows into the dataset.

In the business context, k-folds ensembling can help companies make more accurate forecasts, be it for sales, customer churn, or prices. It's using the team of analysts who each bring their unique perspective, and then combining their insights for a more balanced and accurate view. The initial gains from ensembling multiple models can be substantial. For instance, the ensemble model might be far less prone to overfitting and could generalize much better to new, unseen data. However, as you keep adding more and more models into the ensemble, the incremental benefits tend to diminish.

Suppose the performance is measured using the silhouette score, a metric that ranges from -1 to 1, with higher scores indicating better clustering. When using a single customer model, the silhouette score might be 0.60. However, the performance significantly improves to 0.75 when ensembling two models, yielding a substantial improvement of 0.15. As more models are added to the ensemble, the performance continues to improve but at a decreasing rate. For instance, when the ensemble is expanded to include 50 models, the silhouette score reaches 0.80, an improvement of just 0.05 from using two models. Adding a 51st model to this ensemble yields a score of 0.81, offering a marginal gain of only 0.01.

This is a rough example of diminishing returns for model en-

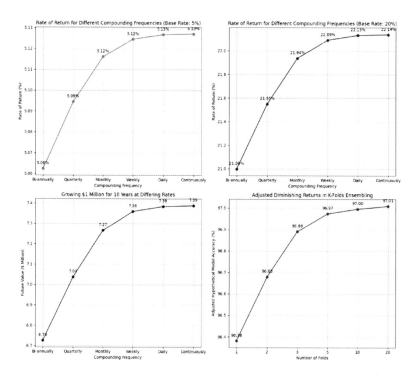

Figure 9.2: Continuous compounding and k-folds ensembling both encounter diminishing returns by exhausting a reservoir.

sembling. The initial addition of a second model to the ensemble leads to a significant performance boost, but subsequent additions provide incrementally smaller benefits. Therefore, it's crucial to consider the tradeoff between computational resources and performance gains when deciding the number of models to include in an ensemble.

In a deeper sense, diminishing returns occur when repeatedly tapping into a limited resource. For a familiar example, compounding involves earning interest on both the principal amount and the interest that has been accrued (fig. 9.2). Continuous compounding refers to the mathematical limit where interest is calculated and added back to the principal continuously, as opposed to being calculated at discrete intervals (e.g., annually, semi-annually). Initially, the impact can be substantial as the growth rate increases. However, the rate of return starts to plateau as time goes on.

Like k-folds ensembling, the initial impact of compounding can be substantial. However, as you exhaust the reservoir, the improvement rate plateaus. In both cases, understanding the cause of diminishing returns can help in resource allocation. For k-folds ensembling, knowing when to stop adding more models can save computational resources and time. In finance, understanding the effects of continuous compounding can influence investment decisions, when to double up or diversify.

9.5 Testing Man And Machine

Running a quantitative fund, man and machine reach their highest art. The man-machine interface has gripped strategic thinkers since the contest between Deep Blue and Kasparov. The story starts there. MIT's Erik Brynjolfsson and Andrew McAfee provide a modern update in their book, "The Second Machine Age". Besides inventing the metaphor of AI being as transformative as the advent of electricity, they write:

> The teams of human plus machine dominated even the strongest computers... Human strategic guidance combined with the tactical acuity of a computer was overwhelming. The surprise came at the conclusion of the event. The winner was revealed to be not a grandmaster with a state-of-the-art PC but a pair of amateur American chess players using three computers at the same time.

– Chapter 12, Learning To Race With Machines

The man-machine combination can dominate. New research from Stanford University considers data sources to explain how AI systems can counteract bias in decision making, an important step in taming Keynes' animal spirits. They examined how human decisions vary when augmented with a system that could ingest data they hadn't considered.[16]

Like the example of Munger's man in China, the very best managers have resources for comprehensive coverage of data. The researcher's work examined coverage by adding or subtracting factors available to a human using an ML system. The remarkable work shows just how knowledge is power when it comes to decision making. When coverage was reduced, the animal spirits in the decision makers were unleashed, meaning increased bias. They identified four main regimes in their study (fig. 9.3).

When there is a substantial true difference between groups, ML algos that include group information in their calculations tend to be more accurate than those that do not. In such a context, incorporating group identity in predictive models offers an advantage in prediction accuracy. Interestingly, the typical tradeoff between accuracy and disparity can undergo a reversal under certain conditions. Specifically, if the human decision-maker responsible for interpreting or acting on the predictions has a bias that leads them to overestimate differences between groups, incorporating both the machine's prediction and the human bias can actually negate this tradeoff. In these instances, accounting for human bias while making data-driven decisions can result in both high accuracy and low bias between groups.

On the flip side, when the true difference between groups is minimal, ML predictions that do not consider group information are generally as accurate as those that do. In this so-called dominance regime, ignoring group identity may be an appropriate, as it doesn't adversely affect the algorithm's predictive accuracy.

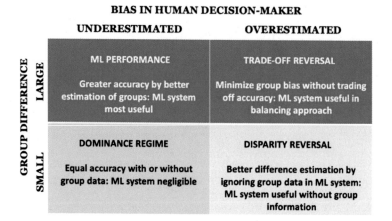

Figure 9.3: Group difference and bias regimes indicate effectiveness of combined AI-human decision frameworks

Of course, this ex-post analysis isn't always available at the outset.

In scenarios where a human decision-maker has a bias that artificially amplifies the differences between groups, ML algos that don't account for group identity can counteract this bias. This phenomenon, known as disparity reversal, stands in contrast to the conventional wisdom that including group information in predictive models increases both disparity and accuracy. In such cases, omitting group information can lead to more equitable outcomes without sacrificing predictive accuracy.

In context of machine-assisted human decision-making, incorporating group information in prediction changes from the direct implementation of machine predictions. Specifically, when decision-makers have biases, machine-assisted predictions that account for group differences can help overcome these biases and improve decision accuracy, but with a special case when there are small overestimations of group differences.

168

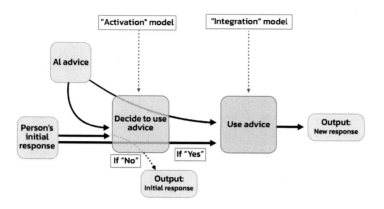

Figure 9.4: Stanford Activation-Integration model for human AI interaction[74]

Let's phrase in terms of market scenarios and valuations. In the scenarios, the general idea is that considering the correct level of group (sector, asset metric, etc.) information can help achieve more accurate and fair valuations. However, the right approach depends on the actual level of disparity and whether humans tend to underestimate or overestimate it.

The whole exercise suggests we must look beyond the algorithms themselves and consider the whole decision-making environment, including how the algorithms inform human decision-making, to truly address bias and fairness. It also highlights that traditional strategies to ensure focus, such as excluding certain types of data, might not work as expected when human decision-makers are involved.

A different Stanford group considered exactly human AI decision-making together. Their activation-integration model (Fig. 9.4) shows two modes of activation, where the decision maker has processed the advice and integration where the AI advice has been incorporated. The researchers used a trained model based on thousands of human-AI interactions to determine how to adjust the AI's predicted confidence levels. This altered AI confidence, although technically uncalibrated, aimed to improve the final decision made by the human participant. While their results are preliminary, they studied the diagnosis of difficult medical cases. Empirical validation of the research was conducted across a variety of tasks, including image, text, and tabular data. They studied hundreds of participants to support their hypothesis increased AI confidence led to more accurate human predictions and decisions, irrespective of the task type. Their work is a sequential step to shape the regimes discussed earlier.

Optimizing AI advice according to human interaction opens up exciting avenues for improving human-AI collaboration. When AI is integrated into systems where humans are the end users, the optimization of AI should not be done in isolation. It's fitting that AI trained to absorb the better nature of its human masters, may in the end, help resolve the animal spirits that lie within.

9.6 The Engineering Discipline

What does the Manhattan Project have to do with exponential returns? Innovation at its basic level means creating world-changing capability. Like the Manhattan Project, the Nvidia way implemented by Huang fosters an open technical society. Big tech and the methods to achieve it have more in common with the Manhattan Project than with Bell Labs, the corporate R&D Eden. The two books, "American Prometheus" and "The Idea Factory", describe the historical milieu of each. Only the Manhattan Project corralled the best scientific groups in open exchange towards a complete product.

At Nvidia, Huang instituted an engineering-wide distribution list, the ML alias, where the best technical engineers evaluated new development and techniques. Like the charismatic J. Robert

Oppenheimer, Huang knew when the boss' touch could stimulate discussion or turn an unproductive avenue. Huang cultivated the collaboration of top tier technical minds bent in common purpose as the way to usher transformative technologies. Huang's Nvidia is responsible for not one, but two exponential breakthroughs. First with visual computing and second with parallel computing power lifting the level of creativity and intelligence.

How far was Huang willing to go in pursuit of engineering excellence and thorough understanding? Huang instituted an internal GPU cloud, mirroring the capability available from Amazon Web Services as cloud computing. Huang invested resources in deploying a GPU cloud computing service as an internal service without any intention of releasing the compute to the general public. First, it would've been foolhardy to enter in the slugfest between Google, Amazon, Microsoft, and even a host of startups. Instead, Huang kept all of these cloud companies as his customers. Yet, he valued the customer relationship and engineering competency such that he wouldn't let his engineers lag at the drafting table. Engineers know working deeply with a problem means holding the parts in your working memory. As Hinton alluded, holding a concept in memory causes the work to change our biological hardware, our brain neurons.[42] Huang is a man who always pays his technical debts. Huang, through his actions, impressed the Nvidia culture unto legions of new hires without the hubris of ill-aimed moonshots.

Bell Labs, as related in "The Idea Factory", gave unparalleled freedom to small groups of enormous talent. This is the strategy known in Google as "let a thousand flowers bloom". Such a strategy is vulnerable to spillovers, letting others pick the bouquet. The Nvidia way is to never rest and strive to grow the moat at every opportunity. Advancements such as the transistor, fiber optics, solar cells emerged, but without AT&T reaping the rewards by completing development. Bell Labs lacked the talented director to turn creative exploration to common purpose and mission. In some part, our purpose is not to merely adopt AI, but to join towards exponential progress.

10 Generative AI: Usage Patterns and Emerging Tools

In the film "AI", Steven Spielberg directs the touching account an embodied AI (played by Haley Joel Osment) with the capacity for love. In a case of life imitating art, the emphasis of alignment to produce emergent phenomenon in RL has made fiction closer to fact. Let's revisit Wittgenstein's examination of language.

The philosophy of Wittgenstein drives home the mechanisms of how OpenAI has succeeded with RL. Wittgenstein is the famous proponent of the language-game framework, in short the context of words and actions that surround the real use of language. This turn of the century philosopher and contemporary with the great Alan Turing is notably insightful. The life of Wittgenstein echoes the parable of the Green Knight.

As a precocious genius, Wittgenstein was raised with the cultural elite of Vienna as afforded by a captain of industry patriarch. He continued seeking the best teachers, landing on Bertrand Russell's doorstep to launch his philosophy career. Like the personage who first inspired koans, Wittgenstein gave up family fortune to think deeply by retreating to the desolate Norwegian landscape. Only after his retreat during which he inconceivably spent years as a primary school teacher, did he subject himself to the trials and tribulations that led him to discard the triumph of his graduate thesis, "Tractatus Logico-Philosophicus", in favor of his post-humous volume "Philosophical Investigations".

His goal in Investigations is stated as:

> What is your aim in philosophy? –To show the fly
> the way out of the fly bottle.
>   – §309. Philosophical Investigations

"Philosophical Investigations" reads as a collection of first principles koans than a traditional logical elucidation. As first described by Hofstadter's "Gödel, Escher, Bach", koans act as a paradigm-shattering inducement to break through the (Gödel) Incompleteness of axiomatic thought, such as the language dimensions that form the explanation of a business thesis. Wittgenstein's work prescribes a path forward for the development of one pillar of general intelligence (in concert with the External World problem and Other Minds paradigm).

Tasks characteristic of language games are Question and Answering in Context [75] and other multi-round interactions centered on learning. [76] Prior to the training recipe of ChatGPT, LLMs fell short in the interactive learning tasks of language use. The training recipe of ChatGPT takes the base capability of fluency created through causal language modeling and emphasizes instruction following, known in short-hand as fidelity (to the user's instructions). [55]

10.1 Causal Language Modeling

Contrary to its wunderkind behavior, AI is built up like a layer cake. First, a base level of diction is created. Far from being trivial, progress through diction dominated all the way into the advent of generative AI (ChatGPT). The linguist Sir J.R. Firth's pronouncement, "you shall know a word by the company it keeps", becomes nearly a cliché. This fluency capability is trained through causal language modeling and takes up the majority of computation. Causal language modeling is a straightforward process where a LLM is shown some sequence of text and then trained to give a prediction of the next word. Several recent descriptions have stopped here as the explanation of generative AI. It's important to bust the myth that generative AI is merely next word prediction – this merely sets the stage. However, the real marvel lies in scaling these models for internet-wide applications. DeepMind researchers point out that language models learn from community discussions online. It doesn't make sense to compare the intelligence from an LLM to a single person, and instead the correct comparison is the capture of a community or culture. In studies of the input datasets, DeepMind researchers identified the dataset had to have a Zipfian distribution.[49] Essentially, the dataset had to have a sufficient number of rare topics. Increasing the label multiplicity, the number of labels per class, increased the ability of LLMs to adapt to user requests without retraining, a process known as in-context learning. We had discussed earlier that the Chinese internet, being a closed and censored culture, lacks the discourse that is a precondition for scaling LLMs. Strangely, many Chinese researchers in private discussions understood this intuitively ahead of the quantitative research from DeepMind. Censorship has a chilling effect on innovation.

10.2 Generative Modeling

Causal language modeling had been a long effort from scientists, and OpenAI had a key insight that paved their path to GPT-3 (the ChatGPT predecessor). Remarkably, their insight connected to Munger's favorite mathematician catch-phrase, "invert, always invert " (man muss immer umkehren), originally from Jacobi. OpenAI emphasized so-called decoder only casual language modeling. Before, scientists used an encoder portion, which created a mapping of many to one (vector representation), and then the decoder took the one vector to many (words). OpenAI's insight was counter-intuitive and a bolt of clarity because it stripped the neural network, yet increased modeling power. Seemingly, they took one step back on architectural complexity to take two steps forward in expressivity. By using only a decoder neural network, they matched the many to one mapping to the expressive generative problem. They worked from their desired result, and inverted to settle on the correct architecture, even when prevailing practice suggested otherwise. Their achievement rocked the scientific establishment when they published their GPT-3 paper, "Language Models are Few-Shot Learners".

10.3 Reward Model Loop

Earlier we discussed the tension between the encoder and decoder, couched in terms of the Platonic ideal and instantiations of the ideal. Generative AI architectures are typically decoder only with the reward model (RM) handling some of the conceptual burden typically handled by the encoder. In RL, an agent interacts with an environment to achieve a certain goal. The agent takes actions based on its current state and receives rewards from the environment in return. The goal of the agent is to learn a policy that maximizes the expected sum of rewards over time. The RM is the function that quantifies the desirability of the states that the agent can encounter. Scientists struggled with absorbing the best parts of RL (the RM) into NLU. As an old martial arts teacher liked to say, it wasn't practice that made perfect, rather perfect practice that made perfect. In the ML language, a meta-learning approach to the learning process is necessary to reach new heights. The RM is exactly the step that takes causal LM and grades it for human preferences.

The design of the RM is critical for the agent's performance and learning efficiency. Sparse and dense rewards represent two ends of a spectrum. With sparse rewards, the agent receives feedback only upon achieving the end goal, making the task more challenging but potentially more interesting. Dense rewards, on the other hand, offer feedback at each step, which generally accelerates the learning process but may not always lead to the most optimal or interesting solutions.

The reward function should both incentivize good behavior and penalize bad behavior. Positive rewards can be assigned for actions that move the agent closer to its goal, such as reaching a particular location or acquiring an item. Conversely, negative rewards can be used to discourage actions that lead to failure or undesirable states, like hitting a wall, falling off a cliff, or spouting nonsense.

In situations where multiple behaviors or outcomes are desirable, a tradeoff may be necessary. This can be achieved by assigning different weights to different types of rewards. For instance, reaching the end goal might carry more weight than avoiding obstacles. However, striking a balance is crucial to prevent the agent from learning suboptimal behavior or overfitting to the training set.

First, the RM is trained to discern between a generated output and human text and issue a rating from zero to nine. RM training follows these steps:

- Collect data: The language model responds to a variety of prompts and questions.

- Rate data: Human experts review generated responses and human responses and rate them based on a rubric. In particular, OpenAI went to lengths to create a 7 point Likert (psychometric) scale to replicate the essence of following instructions[55]

- Train reward model: Using the expert ratings, the RM is

trained to help the LLM understand desirable responses. The RM mimics the human labelers calculating a rating as the reward factor for the RL model during training

The RM captures desired semantic qualities that can be hard capture with hand-designed criteria. Humans often have criteria they find difficult to express. Radiologists use a special term, "Aunt Minnie", that captures the ineffability of their job. When a radiologist at the University of Cincinnati was pressed on what he saw in a radiograph that caused his diagnosis, he stated, that it was as clear to him as if his Aunt Minnie was in the radiograph. The first RM trained by OpenAI captured the semantics of a good summary using a ten point scale across several dimensions. Their release of ChatGPT expanded their RM to question and answering, brainstorming, chatting, rewriting, classification, and open-ended generation.[55] They furthered scaled instruction tasks with the GPT-4 arguably achieving semantic capture of generic instruction following. Instruction following as a generic mandate is strong. For example, some detractors said that GPT-4 can't write jokes. When asked to extend a joke from Mervyn King's book, GPT-4 added:

> A physicist, a chemist, and an economist are stranded on a desert island with a can of food. They need to find a way to open it.
>
> The physicist says, "We can use the principle of leverage. If we find a suitable fulcrum and a sturdy lever, we can pry the can open with minimal effort."
>
> The chemist chimes in, "Or we could find a reactive substance on the island and create a chemical reaction to dissolve the can's seal, making it easy to open."
>
> The economist, rubbing his chin thoughtfully, finally speaks up, "You're both overcomplicating things. Let's just assume we have a can opener."

> GPT-4: The mathematician then adds, "Actually, there's a more elegant solution. We can prove that the can is open by contradiction. First, let's assume the can is not open..."

If GPT-4 hasn't reached the high art of original jokes, it can at least extend jokes as a theme. By some historian accounts, humanity domesticated canids 23,000 years ago. Canids live to please their human caretakers with an almost infinite capability to read emotions. As the domestication of canids occurred in pre-history, historians aren't exactly sure how dogs became man's best friend. Anthropologists surmise that increasing expansion of human habitats lead to frequent positive encounters, which then lead to an ever escalating co-habitation. Generative AI is now in the period where AI lives with humanity. In OpenAI's terminology, RMs capture the nature of instruction following. The process has now started for co-evolution and mutual productivity. While right now GPT-4 dominates the benchmarks, the research community has revealed early hints on how alignment will evolve. An umbrella concern is that generative AI is often all too eager to please (the junior developer Earnest). We discuss methods to adjust this behavior. Like canids, there are a plethora of breeds and dispositions that fit different situations.

10.4 PPO: The Core Training

It's worth examining exactly how the RM is used in training generative AI, the so-called PPO (Proximal Policy Optimization) RL loop. Surprisingly, we've already assembled the pieces. Fundamentally, PPO comprises of two key components, the policy model and the value model. In simple terms, the policy model suggests the next word, and the value model assesses the quality. As you might infer, the value model is the RM we introduced earlier, and where our human judgement comes in. The policy model is exactly the fluency model, the decoder-based architecture.

RL mimics the processes of biological organisms. Unexpectedly, the struggle to learn is the same for the living and the silicon – when should a strategy be maintained and when should new methods be explored? The answer is convergent. Phases of exploration and exploitation should be interleaved. On the human front, Steven Kotler chronicles the millennia-old practice of shattering ossified thinking patterns in his text, "Stealing Fire". Luckily for AI agents, exploration can be switched on cyclically via swapping in a different reward signal. Recent work from Stanford Education Professor Nick Haber's laboratory added an elegant solution, making agents curious.[77] In contrast to previous approaches, their Curious Replay approach uses curiosity as a guiding force, not for making decisions, but for selecting experiences to learn from. This curiosity-driven method improves AI performance in environments that undergo changes, while still maintaining effectiveness in stable environments.

Agent curiosity is beneficial in less obvious adaptation scenarios, like in an open-world game called Crafter. One key understanding behind Curious Replay is that an AI model needs to keep up with environmental changes to function effectively. If an AI model is inaccurate or outdated, it can make poor decisions, especially when encountering new situations, leading to a downward spiral of bad decision-making and data collection. This hints at the broad potential of this method in improving AI adaptability in a variety of situations.

Curious Replay addresses this by focusing the AI's learning on the unfamiliar or challenging parts of its environment. This is a big shift from how AI usually learns, which is by randomly revisiting old experiences. This older approach can lead to AI focusing too much on experiences that are no longer relevant, and missing out on key updates to its understanding of the world.

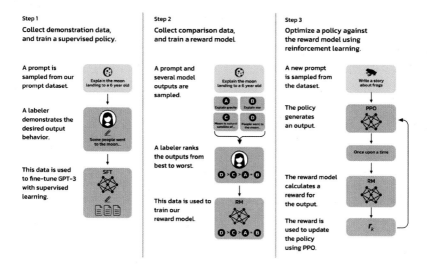

Figure 10.1: Reinforcement Learning from Human Feedback (RLHF) incorporates the Reward Model (RM) and the LLM in a PPO loop.

Building on the success of a technique called prioritized experience replay, Curious Replay further refines it by introducing curiosity into the equation, resulting in a significant leap in AI adaptability. Curious Replay improves AI performance in new tests, with a six-fold increase in object interaction tasks.

The RL loop balances fast learning with thorough understanding by iterating LLM predictions and RM ratings. Like Bayesian modeling, it's important to update beliefs as new evidence becomes available. The NN update is extremely powerful with all pieces assembled (fig. 10.1). We have finally unveiled the paradigm of RLHF.

By combining RL with generative GPT-based architectures, every word is subject to a Bayesian update, meaning human feedback trains the NN at every single utterance. Imagine listening critically to a speaker and hanging on every single word uttered. One single wrong word can disrupt the entire message. We've all had this experience listening to speeches, hanging on every word. RLHF has effectively recreated it. Every word matters – that's the level of precision RLHF brings to the table.

10.5 Teaching AI

We completed a detailed description of generative AI creation for good reason. Understanding mechanisms allow inductive leaps in our use, deployment, and expectations. We collect the surprising insight – teaching AI is similar to teaching humans. At every step of the process, the good teacher reduces inductive leaps for the student until the student is ready to take them (similarly to the RLHF process, the overall goal is to follow instructions). The celebrated Professor Joseph Chang at Yale Statistics was a master at setting the level for the student. More than a decade later, I can still remember Professor Chang breaking down a three state Markov process to discuss the equilibrium state. To be more accurate, he didn't reveal the answer, he brought me to the point where I could reveal the answer for myself. We proceed with reducing gaps in expected results as we discuss prompting and Bayesian inference.

10.6 Prompting Strategies

For humans, asking a general question usually elicits a general answer. Heath, the Stanford business school professor, explains that humans tend to activate their brains in different modes.[48] For instance, citing statistics will prompt humans to start estimating figures. Remarkably, there's some evidence to suggest that prompting LLMs is similar, activating subnetworks that are specialized for tasks.[78;79] For humans, switching brain modes or multi-tasking is difficult. Recent research first had to reveal that since humans have one brain, true multi-tasking isn't possible. Multitasking is really switching brain modes sequentially. Professor Cal Newport, the author of "Deep Work", notes multi-tasking degrades performance on tasks due to an attention residue that lingers between tasks.[33] Changing contexts for an LLM is as easy as initiating a new session, allowing the user to stay at a high level. When we frame using LLMs in terms of activating subnetworks, we can effectively access the latent knowledge contained in the generative LLM. That makes it easier to accomplish tasks by reducing cognitive load and context switching. Why do most people find it easier to manage a project rather than execute it? It's not just that more work has to be done. There's painful context switch from planning to execution. In fact, planning is so different that we've all experienced starting a project but requiring guidance and feedback to create the structure of a good presentation or report. Prompt engineering allows a democratization of management. LLMs have made its users into managers in the new AI age.

While in the planning context, it especially makes sense to use generative AI. By staying in the planning context when using LLMs for planning, and it forms the super structure for the task. The first problem is that the LLM can be too good at generating ideas, rattling on and on. One tip from Dally addresses this. Dally, well-aware of the importance of the planning context, makes a list of tasks for the day. Then, he immediately draws a line. All tasks underneath the line he just concedes they won't be done. For him, he refines the planning stage by immediately balancing the need to get things done in an effective display of essentialism.

Newport analyzes executive Jack Dorsey, sketching out a character who doesn't engage in deep work, rather seeking to manage many contexts. Newport exactly hits on the usage mode of

LLMs. When you use generative AI, you are Jensen Huang, Jack Welch, Henry Singleton, Gordon Moore, or Andy Grove. You have access to a broad and deep company of talented agents. Only you have to be in the frame to use it. How do we find the proper frame?

A Carnegie Mellon University study revealed that charity donors gave less on average when they were inundated with statistics.[80] Unexpectedly, generative AI seems to get overwhelmed by information, forgetting instructions when they're chained together. This can be frustrating because the AI behaves more like a scatterbrain than the advanced agent it's supposed to be. The frustration is compounded because ChatGPT, especially GPT-4 versions and later, is capable of superhuman feats. Sometimes, even talented actors need to be directed in the right direction.

10.7 Moving Ahead of The Quants

Generative AI, forged at the intersection of the sciences and humanities, allows the shocking result of leapfrogging the quants. Several quant practices are rooted in common sense that value investors recognize, for instance controlling risk and understanding tradeoffs. Quants use the practice of bootstrapping to simulate different possible trajectories in the past. Bootstrapping is a creative way of rearranging historical financial prices to guess how things might behave in the future. Think of it as taking a film of past investment performance, cutting it into smaller clips, and then shuffling those clips to create a new film. Each clip (block) has a fixed length but starts at a random point in the original film. By doing this, it acknowledges that investments can be unpredictable and don't always follow past patterns. This rearranging helps construct a new series of possible future returns, giving a better understanding of potential investment behaviors without just assuming they'll do exactly what they did in the past.

It that strikes as slightly nonsensical, it is. Usually by sampling from the time course, it makes the assumption of the source distribution as a prior belief. The problem with that is we can easily imagine time courses with markedly different trajectories. For instance, the evolution of horizontal and vertical integration in business is a potent study across economies. Like a growing crystal lattice, the dominant companies of different nations often fall into different niches and solidify their advantage. Where there's Facebook in the US, China has WeChat. Moreover, WhatsApp and Facebook combined don't replicate the same app of apps functionality in WeChat. Where Latin America has MercadoLibre, the US has two separate companies in Amazon and PayPal, not to mention AWS, which most businesses wouldn't attempt. In Mexico, Fomento Económico Mexicano is a vertically integrated brewer, bottler, and gas station chain replicating Coca Cola (where they own a large stake of the Mexican business), Casey's General Store, and Heineken (which they divested) all wrapped in one. If even different economies evolved with incredible diversity, then domestic self-sampling bootstrapping can't simulate the multiverse.

Generative AI is an interactive technology that reflects the user as much as the community, permitting scenarios only bounded by the creativity of the questioner. This is particularly useful for Bayesian updates considering counterfactual worlds (sec. 3.8). The lone investor can rapidly and intuitively hone generative bootstrapping (counterfactual modeling). Generative bootstrapping plays out materially different scenarios and then submits those as possible inputs to the rest of the due diligence pipeline. For both quants and value investors, generative bootstrapping marks a robust process.

10.8 Asking the Right Question

Prompt engineering, the art of asking generative AI the right question, has drawn ridicule. Yet industry scions say prompt engineers will have the last laugh. [81] President Lincoln proclaimed, "give me six hours to chop down a tree and I will spend the first four sharpening the axe." Einstein echoed "if had an hour to solve a problem and my life depended on the solution, 1 would spend the first 55 minutes determining the proper question to ask for once I know the proper question, 1 could solve the problem in less than five minutes." The polymath George Pólya taught this in his manual, "How to Solve It". He presents a general approach to solving problems that can be applied to logical problems. We find that his methods can be implemented with AI.

Pólya's method isn't complex. First, Pólya says you need to understand the problem, taking a moment to really get what's going on. You want to know what you're being asked, what information you've got, and what you're trying to find out. Imagine if someone tossed you a puzzle and said, "Solve this!" You'd want to look it over, turn the pieces around in your hands, and figure out what picture you're trying to make before you dove in. Occasionally, the market serves up a puzzle. Are certain trends early, mid, or late cycle? What are the risks involved? What's the market like right now? It's about asking the right questions to figure out what exactly you're dealing with, just like a logic problem. We covered looking at financial filings and management performance. You'd ask questions like, "Does this company have a durable moat?", "What's the potential growth?", and "What's the worst case?" The right questions create a roadmap. Studying innovation, Columbia Professor Sheena Iyengar relates that brainstorming is bringing out the sum total of experience in participants, and there is much experience to plumb with generative AI. [82]

Elevate Pólya's process with generative AI by asking the right questions. Asking the right questions isn't easy, even when the puzzle is present. A common event in a science olympiad is the "Write It, Do It" event. In the event, a teammate is asked for instructions to reconstruct a structure from raw materials. The second teammate must construct the object without ever having read the instructions. The exercise is curiously difficult. The first teammate must anticipate the right questions. The second teammate must apply consistent conceptual frameworks devised earlier. For investing, sometimes the pari-mutuel nature of markets imitates a game of "Write It, Do It".

Next, he says to devise a plan. Don't just wing it and hope for the best. Figure out a way to tackle the problem. Once you've devised the plan, execute it. Invest according to the intrinsic value identified. Again, asking the right questions along the way helps you stay on track. Is it still a good investment? Have the fundamentals changed? Follow your plan without preconceived notions. Sometimes it's smooth sailing, other times there's rough waters. If there's a snag, perform a Bayesian update as we've discussed, considering counterfactual worlds to your original hypothesis. We present a strategic plan example in sec. 11.2.

Finally, Pólya says review what you've done. Reflect on it. See if it makes sense. When the puzzle's assembled, view it – is there a consistent conceptual framework? You're looking back at your investments, seeing what worked, what didn't, and learning from it. Why did this investment perform this way? What can be done differently next time. Check the work to make sure it's solid, and meditate on it such that the method springs forth effortlessly the next time a similar problem occurs.

AI takes these steps and supercharges them. Take the reflection step. If you need a financial analyst, it conjures one. It sifts through vast datasets rapidly, helping understand the problem faster and with more depth. It can devise more nuanced and adaptable plans by uncovering hidden patterns and correlations.

Genius often manifests as the precocious prodigy. Those who study geniuses like Mozart understand that a comprehensive teacher, in Mozart's case his father, instills what computer scientists call the right inductive bias. Geniuses have an eerie taste for the next step, the next progression that will elevate their work. For the rest of us without an ever-present mentor, we can slot in generative AI.

Pólya's way of thinking isn't just about solving puzzles. It's a way to approach complexity, especially prevalent in modern investing. And with the help of generative AI, it's not just about doing things faster or on a bigger scale; it's about executing with insight. Knowing what questions to ask and having the tools to find the answers is a sea change. The rise of prompt engineering signifies knowledge workers are generating wisdom.

10.9 Emergent Behavior

In Stephen Wolfram's exploratory AI book, "A New Kind of Science", he details the Game of Life, a two dimensional board of flowing pixel blocks that change based on simple rules. The beautiful patterns and generations tantalized computer scientists. The programmers were dazzled by emergent phenomena, life-like behavior that arose from simple instruction. My high school biology teacher Edgar Boucher used a subtle demonstration to disrupt concepts of life. Boucher projected a blob that seemed to eat other blobs as well as divide under stimuli. Inspecting the projector revealed the blob was merely a drop of mercury responding to chemical stimuli. Life, intelligence, and value investing is beyond simple rules.

When we discussed RLHF, we understood how the evolution of fixed rules were sharpened to capture the high-level concept of following instructions. Urging a system to follow instructions, subsumes and elevates many desired behaviors across many levels of human knowledge work. In a way, instruction following, which we know from student and teacher experiences, has core meta-learning functionality. By integrating instruction-following with Bayesian inference, we establish a usage pattern for generative AI.

If we want to use generative AI effectively, we bundle context information succinctly. Anthropologists describe these bundles as cultural knowledge. For instance, describing liberty and freedom to most Americans would conjure up a powerful mix of associations that places the American in a frame of mind. Generative AI is a technology built of a literate society for a literate society. The masters of generative AI move like master CEOs, able to shift from frame to frame, managing different contexts to the utmost capability. It's not exactly a comfortable feeling for most people, but just like there are expert executives, there are managers that excel at it.

Every generative AI user is now a manager of colossal institutional knowledge, that of an open and free society. The established business literature remote to the rank-and-file worker is now accessible. While OpenAI has started the democratization of AI, much work remains.

10.10 Ability Limits

There are surprising instances where GPT-4 doesn't perform well. In OpenAI's technical overview, the writing benchmark is at the 54th percentile of GRE test takers. Writing seems the very embodiment of generative function, generating words. Why the shortfall?

Our tools of Bayesian inference and RLHF mechanisms equip us to understand the limits of GPT-4 for writing. Good writing is a generation of text and a critique of writing at the same time.

Anyone who has graded college papers knows the headache of students that haven't taken the time to read their own writing. More critique is better in the oft-used phrase "good writing is re-writing" and Hemingway even going as far as "the only kind of writing is rewriting". Generative AI out of the box doesn't write well, having a voice that reverts to the mean.

Bayesian inference means that generative AI is bound to the context that birthed it. RLHF means generative AI is the repository of online conversational knowledge. Writing mimics the community from whence it's drawn. Just as communities are varied, voice can vary leading to uneven tone, another demerit on the writing scorecard. Now as a flexible tool, numerous frameworks have emerged to shape the prior prompt. Sophisticated prompt engineering can wring performance, though it's a meticulous task. On the other hand, the GPT-4 benchmark for AP macroeconomics was top marks at 84th percentile, meaning some tasks are well captured.[83]

Architecture imposes stricter ability limits. We discussed how the decoder-only architecture is optimized for generation. If a many to one judgement is required, then the generative architecture isn't suitable. Alternatively, encoder-decoder architectures specializes in taking the many-fold branching of a natural sequence into a single point estimation. We use encoder-decoder architectures for securities ranking.

10.11 Model Explainability: The Nonbeliever's Crutch?

Model explainability for large ML models brings a Catch-22. Doesn't model explainability simplify the large-scale analysis to the point of omission? Put another way, what's the point of asking the model to explain itself if the purpose is to achieve performance without sacrificing details. Startlingly, we find model explainability has a two-fold purpose – first, it gives the opportunity to impress, and second, like the kanban methods of the Toyota Way, it monitors proper function in the factory (engine) of assembly.

Demis Hassabis, co-founder of Deepmind, recounts the 37th move of his world champion AlphaGo AI. The so-called God move stunned the world with its creativeness and piercing insight. A human grandmaster would've made such a move only 1 in 10,000 games.[84] The move staggered the human World Champion, Lee Sedol, crushing his morale with its deliberateness. Similarly, we've found that using AI for financial analysis has equal moments of brilliance with one important caveat – generative AI is not enough.

As we mentioned, we use encoder-decoder architectures for securities rankings. However, for our kanban purposes (data visualization for engine monitoring), we augment with generative AI. We specifically tested generative AI on its own for securities rankings and it didn't match up to a well-executed ensemble (fig. 10.2). However, when generative AI is used for model explainability in concert with an ensemble model, the results are dramatic. Take the case of generative AI (ChatGPT) alone for securities ranking (A) and then (B) used with the ensemble model to explain the results:

(A) Grade: B. Confidence: 0.8. Market Axess Holdings Inc. has a strong business model with a leading electronic trading platform in fixed-income markets. The company has consistently paid dividends and has authorized multiple share repurchase programs. However, the lack of information on intrinsic value metrics such as free cash flow yield and profit margin makes it difficult to give a higher grade.

(B) Amicus Rating: A. Confidence: 0.6 SLM Corp's Q2 2023 earnings call reveals a robust financial po-

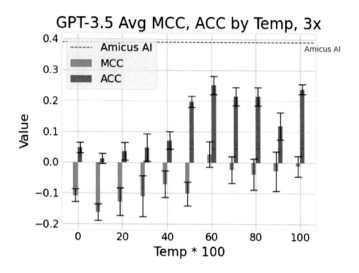

Figure 10.2: (Top) Using ChatGPT 3.5 for securities rankings doesn't perform up to an ensemble method (red line). (Bottom) Testing more recent and powerful models (16k context and GPT-4) don't yield clear improvements either. Each experiment was repeated three times and the standard deviation used as the error bar.

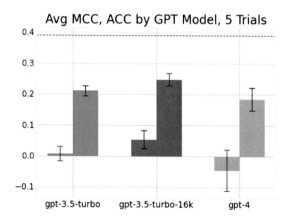

sition. With a successful loan sale of $2 billion at a premium of 6.5% and a 7% reduction in outstanding shares since January 2023, SLM Corp demonstrates strong financial management. Coupled with a 6% increase in private education loan originations, this paints a picture of a company that is not only weathering the storm but thriving in it.

Generative AI alone is both overly confident and non-specific. The model ensemble in concert with generative AI has specific causal explainability that builds human confidence. Generative AI explainability is especially effective on poorly rated securities, likely due to the unique concerns picked out (again Tolstoy's insight, sec. 4.9, unhappy families different). Far from a nonbeliever's crutch, model explainability unifies two modes of AI and elevates their use by humans.

10.12 The Near Future of Generative AI

A client insisted that we focus our analysis on management profiles and motivation. Contrary to popular belief, AI researchers, the ones doing the work, are not driven by power. Consider Y Combinator founder Paul Graham, renowned for his long-form blog posts. His seminal essay "Hackers and Painters" expressed the contrarian idea that (good) software developers and painters are driven by the same urges, as informed by his own forays into the art world at the Rhode Island School of Design. The desire to break the mold, pioneer new modes of expression, with an aesthetic sensibility, encapsulates hackers and painters. Creative people will find new ways of doing things, treating the puzzle as a game. For every game release, a subculture of speed runners emerges based on reading the source code of the game and making it perform to new limits. Prolific Google Brain researcher Quoc Le related he specialized in language models as a graduate student since he wanted a chatty friend. Suppressing the irrepressible creative components of hackers and painters is bottling a revolution. Bottled pressure is rarely a stable configuration.

As Hinton relates, some biological inspirations for AI haven't proved fruitful – his advisee Mengye Ren taking herculean efforts to replicate biological action potentials for marginal gain. [42] The genius of Nvidia CEO Huang's management style inspires the possibilities of generative AI, some projects already in flight. In 2023, Huang described how he manages forty direct reports with no one to one weekly meetings. [14] Of course, Huang states, "None of my management team is coming to me for career advice – they already made it, they're doing great." Huang's reports in 2023 are often CEO's of companies that he has acquired like Mellanox and Parabricks. Huang echoes Buffett's story on Mrs. B, the furniture store founder that couldn't stop executing even in retirement. Executives function at the highest level with minimal coaching. As we've seen from this chapter, we're far from such autonomy with generative AI.

Not to give the wrong impression, Huang's management style involves communication, just at high bandwidth. His meetings with executives pull in senior and key engineers such that business context is shared broadly and concurrently. Generative AI is rapidly improving context sharing through startups like LangChain and LlamaIndex. LlamaIndex provides a vector database. Namely, LlamaIndex organizes a multitude – these could be words, sentences, images, or even entire articles to a system that can quickly and intelligently sort, compare, or find similar items within this collection. A vector embedding database is an efficient filing cabinet for this purpose. Instead of storing these items as they are, the database converts each one into a set of numbers (a vector) that captures its essence or meaning. The closer the vectors are in numerical space, the more similar the original items are. Let's say you're dealing with a collection of fruit. An apple might be converted into a vector like [1, 0.2, 0.8], and a pear into another vector like [0.9, 0.3, 0.7]. In this numerical form, it's easy to see that apples and pears are quite similar (because the numbers in their vectors are close). If you have an orange, represented by a very different vector like [0.2, 0.8, 0.1], then you'd know it's quite different from both apples and pears.

Vector embedding databases are versatile. Whether working with millions of words or thousands of images, the database can quickly find the most similar items or perform other tasks like classification. It's fitting that embeddings, integral in semantic tech, has returned to push AI further again.

11 The Future of Intrinsic Value Investing: Data-Driven Decisions

11.1 Exploration, Exploitation, Values, and Priors

Will AI conquer us and enslave the human race? By now, we've developed some intuition about AI, how it's rooted in ML best practices that seek to distill information to learning in a principled fashion. Here, we tie together some of the analogies for the highest performing investors and ML practitioners. We've drawn parallels from human learning, for instance the constant balance for agents in an exploration or exploitation (deep dive) learning mode. We've now seen that generative AI embodies the culmination of ML work. First, it starts with the foundational TVTP setup as bread and butter with the careful selection of the causal language modeling objective to obtain fluency. Then, followed a series of RLHF steps that drives how hard learning is, and why value investors at their pinnacle will be augmented first, not displaced by AI. These learning principles have been sufficiently general to appeal to a large audience.

The challenge of learning is societal. Every individual and collective struggles to master learning. The physicist and philosopher Fritjof Capra analyzed society as organism in his book, "The Tao of Physics". Social systems are not just the sum of their parts – complex interactions and relationships contribute to the health and sustainability of the whole. Capra presaged George Soros' reflexivity principle (evaluate self-action), which itself appears in physics as the uncertainty principle and hysteresis. Western and Eastern cultures offer different solutions to the learning problem. In essence, culture is a societal prior, a guide to learning. Culture gives us values, which informs the efforts and investments we make. Our collective progress depends on the quality of our learning, our foundational beliefs, and societal values.

11.2 The New Blueprint for Strategic Value Investing: Leveraging AI and Macro Trends

Outperforming markets has never been easy. In the past, investing meant finding bargains in the domestic market. Nowadays, the deluge of information has made generating insights more difficult. At the current competitive level, going from insight to allocation can rigorously benefit from the market opinion. The future of investing combines ML market understanding and global macro analysis in mathematical balance. Investors seeking value can leverage these methods to optimize strategy and methodically approach the market. We present our strategic Blueprint, investing principles and AI powered macro view to conquer modern investing.

Investing in the 21st century blends time-honored principles and advanced technologies. The task hasn't changed – finding undervalued companies using world-class pattern recognition. AI refines the market opinion, the amalgamation of participant views, in two ways. First, AI agents analyze vast amounts of data with a single agent understanding an exponential number of pages a day. They identify subtle patterns too voluminous for human analysts. AI comprehends numerical data in context with qualitative information such as news articles, company reports, and emergent conversational knowledge.

Previously, investing meant searching a small pool of companies that could benefit from growth trends. However, many trends have plateaued and macro effects on companies are complex. An improved approach to value investing is required. Investors must now focus on exponential progress, leveraging AI to correlate thousands of interlocking concepts. AI not only comprehensively understands investing principles, but adapts and learns over time, refining analysis as new data becomes available. Specifically, the benefits are:

- Scale and speed: Parallel processing enables large dataset analysis

- Precision: Quantify subtle patterns in the data, increasing the accuracy of the team's investment decisions

- Global analysis: Gather and analyze in native language sources

- Adaptability: Improve predictions as better methods and data become available

We bind these advantages together with human judgement through (1) an AI mixture of experts ensemble that ranks a target universe of securities, reading financial filings and transcript and modeling a basket of 27 value factors and 31 macro factors (fig. 11.1), and (2) a Bayesian Black-Litterman model to reconcile market correlations and incorporate human macro strategy.[85]

An AI-augmented human better discerns patterns, leveraging empowered processes to refine and optimize investment strategy. Harvard and Stanford research groups have confirmed the power

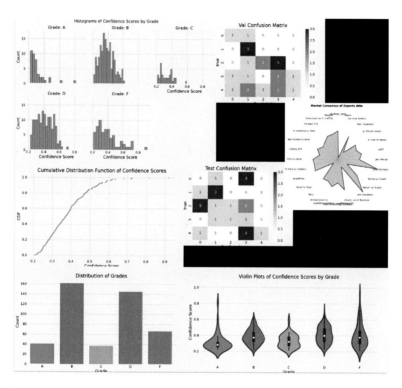

Figure 11.1: Kanban board including factor chart for AI securities rankings

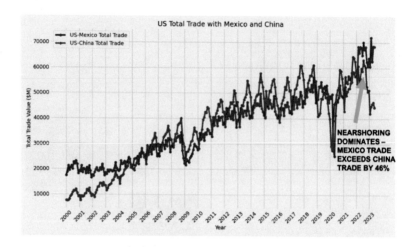

Figure 11.2: Data: US Census Retrieved Aug 12, 2023

of combining human and AI analysis.[16;74;86] What macro view do we combine with our AI agents? The old trends of population, global trade, infrastructure development, and production capacity have reached limits. We're witnessing a shift from exponential to flattening growth in these areas. Population growth is slowing down, commodities extraction is reaching its peak, and government debt is expanding. A plan for the future means understanding new drivers of exponential progress. This is the macro Blueprint to guide AI agents:

Nearshoring: Global geopolitics heating up in anticipation and recognition of hot conflicts has pushed the US towards the old playbook of strengthening NAFTA. The trade shift is dramatic:

Nearshoring has driven Mexican trade to exceed Chinese trade by 46% by July 2023 (fig. 11.2). We believe this trend will persist as geopolitical tensions are unlikely to diminish and even increase.

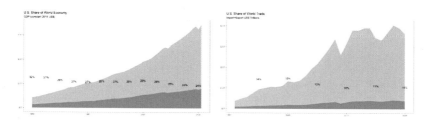

Figure 11.3: U.S. Share of World Economy and World Trade (NY Fed)

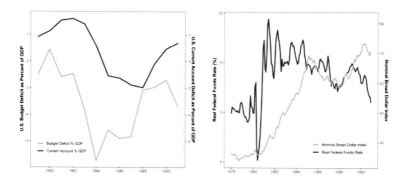

Figure 11.4: US Budget Deficit, Current Account, Interest Rates, and Inflation (NY Fed)

The Dollar's Imperial Circle: Underlying structural demand for US assets occurs as US debt is the primary destination for global savings. Exogenous shocks lead to dollar strength, a phenomenon the Federal Reserve of New York terms the Dollar's Imperial Circle.[87] The knock-on effects include weakening global manufacturing demand due to dollar invoicing and a credit intensive global value chain. Secondary economies that hold rates low while servicing domestic demand benefit their balance of trade. For instance, the Bank of Japan continues to hold its short term rate at -0.1%.[88]

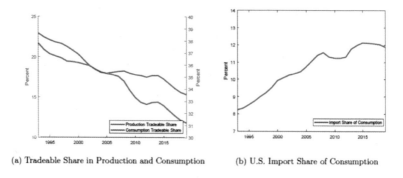

(a) Tradeable Share in Production and Consumption   (b) U.S. Import Share of Consumption

Figure 11.5: (NY Fed)

Negative Trends: Not all trends move in the positive direction. Higher inflation suppressing real growth rates is sticky due to labor shortage. It's vital to hold investments that provide a hedge against negative trends, in addition to identifying positive ones. In healthcare, domestic policy is digesting a cohort of retirees. Some firms will reap the benefits of increased Medicare subscriptions and revenue. Governments will move to inflate away resulting debts while holding rates high for price stability. A company's growth rate must fight the pull from a higher interest rate hurdle, which Buffett likened to gravity.

Labor and Management Dynamics: Labor scarcity leads to increased wages while driving investments in automation (fig. 11.5). Overall, demographic shifts lead to structural transformations in the economy, reducing tradeable share of production and increasing import flow. The synergy or friction between labor and management in this future landscape will define economic growth, requiring an adaptive investment policy.

Global Value Chain: The exogenous shock of a global pandemic has broken and reforged links in the global supply and value chain. Effective coordination between supply chain elements ensures that the right resources are available at the correct

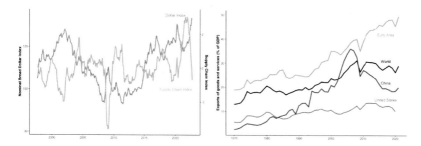

Figure 11.6: Supply Chain Pressure Index and Dollar Index (NY Fed) and Exports of Goods and Services as a Share of GDP (OECD)

time and place, minimizing costs (expanding operating margin) and reducing lead times. Simultaneously, aligning activities of the global value chain delivers competitive advantage (expanding gross margin) in a strong dollar environment. The global supply and value chain are greater than one person or team's understanding, and determining strength is a vital contribution of our AI.

Efficiency: Minimize trading costs, fees, and taxes. Long-term success depends on the exponential rate of growth – drag on this growth rate will erode returns. We implement cost-effective exposure to underlying exponential fundamentals, including appropriate forex carry based on international rate differentials.

These principles are the Blueprint for value investing in the 21st century. This revised approach, combined with an understanding of major global trends, forms the foundation for successful intrinsic value investing in this new era.

Plateauing population growth, expansion of government debt, physical to digital transition, continued technological breakthroughs, and peak in globalization changing labor and management dynamics are the landscape of modern investing. How these trends affect the intrinsic value of companies is core to the Blueprint. The Blueprint understands the new mechanisms driving value to make investments that provide a substantial margin of safety. The Blueprint starts with AI agents ranking companies by intrinsic value, incorporating market valuations as a prior, and then adding global macro views. This adapted approach, which combines AI with a modern understanding of global trends, is the key to success in intrinsic value investing in the 21st century.

Our systems leverage groundbreaking work for a proprietary implementation of deep neural networks for textual data analysis. Our network has over 60 billion neurons, offering superior information coefficients with model explainability. This system allows covering significantly more public companies and data in a fraction of the time. Our systems process over 1.06 billion pages of financial reports, filings, and analyst reports in just nine days – an effort that would take a human analyst 691 years.

However, even with their significant data-processing capabilities, AI tools are not infallible. They complement human insight and judgement for context, interpretation, and ultimately, investment decision-making. This is where the ensemble and Bayesian approach (rigorously using the market opinion) comes into play.

By coupling the extensive analytical abilities of AI with human expertise, we can leverage the best of both worlds. The AI models digest and structure large data sets, while we provide context and interpret results. The Blueprint generates the following portfolio allocations:

Strategic Outlook:

- Strategic emphasis on high growth digital solutions and SaaS platforms that handily exceed peers in a high interest rate environment

- Healthcare follows sustained growth driven by global ag-

Sector	Starting	Amicus Valuation	Final (Leverage 130/30)
Basic Materials	2.2	0.4	2.6
Communication Services	8.7	-8.4	0.4
Consumer Defensive	6.8	5.5	12.3
Consumer Cyclical	10.3	4.8	15.1
Energy	4.2	0.2	4.4
Financial Services	12.0	-12.2	-0.2
Healthcare	13.8	-1.9	11.9
Industrials	8.0	0.9	8.9
Technology	28.6	-6.3	22.3
Real Estate	2.5	-3.3	-0.8
Utilities	2.7	-4.6	-1.9
Global Macro			
Nearshoring	0.0	15.3	15.3
Dollar's Imperial Circle	0.0	9.9	9.9

Figure 11.7: Strategic Blueprint combining AI valuations with ensemble global macro strategy.

ing demographics and ongoing healthcare innovation. As an ongoing government obligation, the sector offers an intrinsic inflation hedge.

- A nearshoring allocation of 15.3% in line with massive geopolitical shifts. The shifts have lasting duration as supply chains are reforged. The elephant will wag the tail for some time to come as US-coupled developing countries absorb capital.

- A foreign industrials, conglomerate, and technology allocation as certain asset values inflate due to the Dollar's Imperial circle

- Investment in Consumer Defensive provides global reach for staples that reach into high growth populations, providing a counterbalancing stability

Tactical Outlook:

- Reduced exposure to Financial Services and negative weight in Investment Banking is a tactical decision to avoid headwinds in the banking sector due to rising interest rates, structural fragility, and regulatory reach

- Hedging allocation to Telecom REITs with expectation of a downturn in broad service economy labor demographics in the near term

- Increased weight in Specialty Chemicals as a tactical move to bank on global manufacturing trends

- Hedging allocation to Media for tactical avoidance of commoditizing streaming technology and market saturation

The Blueprint refines growth-oriented sectors like Technology and defensive sectors like Consumer Staples, with strategy and tactical moves to capitalize on specific industry trends and mitigate potential risks through continuous Bayesian updates. Investing into the future won't be smooth. Comprehensive AI and expert ensembling ensure a durable competitive edge for value at reduced volatility.

11.3 Immediate Development of LLMs

In 1998, Larry Page created the link following algorithm PageRank. He had created the basis of their business, and immediately took a cue from Buffett – went to work building a moat and expanding the moat year by year. What makes a strong moat? The best economic moat example is Munger's exposition on Coca-Cola, the company Buffett has "no desire to go to war with". Munger's canonical example of Coca-Cola centralizes on these points:

1. **Trade secrets**: The formula isn't patented and therefore has the mystique and protection of secrecy

2. **Quality Brand**: Even if the formula could be determined, Coca-Cola globally offers a consistent experience from a remote island to the deepest jungle

3. **Scale**: It is at scale such that even if a rising competitor sought inroads via loss leaders, it'd barely move the needle before said competitor could be acquired or innovation substantially co-opted.

Such factors combine such effect that Buffett states, "If you gave me $100 billion and said, 'Take away the soft drink leadership of Coca-Cola in the world,' I'd give it back to you and say it can't be done". Whereas the Coca-Cola economic moat centers around a physical product, LLMs operates on the great engine of the modern economy, knowledge work and the specialized task.

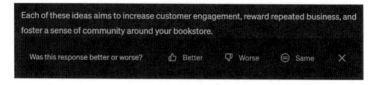

Figure 11.8: OpenAI co-opting the user for data.

We can now map the LLM processes that create economic moats around knowledge products.

1. **Trade secrets through NN architecture and data infrastructure**: even if general techniques in DL are openly shared, the specific implementations and optimizations used by different companies are proprietary, allowing companies who perform well to maintain their advantages.

2. **Quality through quantum leap in performance**: LLM systems have left traditional systems in the dust. AI methods have driven advances that traditionalists previously thought were possible only with decades of work. OpenAI has stayed with its circle of competence. Its ChatGPT plugins leveraged the excitement around LangChain extensions, collecting economic spillovers.

3. **Scale**: As early movers discovered, the more users and data, the better such systems become. Competitors face immense worker hours to create vital data lakes that enable AI systems, not to mention physical datacenter infrastructure. OpenAI is now co-opting Google's old strategy of using user data and soft signals to improve their product (fig. 11.8). They openly use user interactions in their training data via opt-out flow. Oddly, Google identified that when a user stops using your product, it's a strong signal they're satisfied and got what they want.

Though the conditions for AI in enterprise are complex, solutions hinge on laser-focused determination to create a business with an economic moat. As in the example of Coca-Cola, the rewards for successful execution are evident – decades of return and economic premiums. Buffett claims technology is outside his circle of competence, but his mastery of economic moats means his disciples will not be left far behind.

We used the metaphor of generative AI as the direct report Earnest, competent in almost any field. An executive friend negotiated compensation with his executive assistant. Besides avoiding negotiations, the near future of generative AI is that executive assistant functions will improve and immediately empower professionals just in the way the smartphone empowers the masses with the internet in a pocket. An executive assistant is crucial to efficiency, and one skilled in so much is indispensable.

11.4 The Future of Language

Our journey opened with mathematicians that had conquered some aspects of the market. Munger expressed disdain for the algorithmic approach, and many have warned investors away from nerds bearing formulas with good cause. Our surprising view is that they're right. Through the lens of Wittgenstein's work, we discussed a first principles framework of language that reinforces the context-based approach of current AI. We learned that Wittgenstein's language games are a framework towards a more constructive purpose. Like mathematics, language and the games we play with it form an ad-hoc axiomatic construct. It's no surprise that Buffett and Munger, having mastered language games in all of business's permutations, don't need inspiration from mathematics. Most readers could appreciate the limitations mathematics confers as a straitjacket, no matter how precise.

The future of language, bridged by AI, is one where mathematics and language coexist in harmony. Gödel's Incompleteness Theorem, far from showing the limits of mathematicians, enshrines their relevancy. Even concepts as irreducible as the real number system, evolve with new measures such as prime factorizations (p-adic numbers). As language masters, value investors have a brotherhood with mathematicians. The future of business is as many-faceted as the future of humanity. The social animal has a form of commerce since prehistory. Many investors have belabored securities analysis isn't a science. Neither is language, yet each is precise in its own way.

New tools are joining generative AI and mathematics. Researchers from Nvidia and Caltech recently introduced Lean-Dojo,[89] addressing a key issue in theorem proving – premise selection, which is choosing the right base theorem arsenal from a math library to prove a theorem. This is important as the effective selection of premises is vital to reducing complexity.

The authors created a benchmark with almost 100,000 theorems and proofs as a math library. The benchmark is unique because it forces the prover to generalize to theorems that haven't been used in training. When tested, their LLM model performed better than other models and even proved some theorems that currently don't have proofs in existence, demonstrating that this tool can be used to augment math libraries.

Previously, researchers have faced challenges in this field due to private code, data, and significant computational requirements. LeanDojo aims to eliminate these barriers by providing an open-source platform containing tools, data, models, and benchmarks. In the past, tapping into the collaborative power of humanity has had the result of powering forward. Investors will reap the benefits from theorems that flow effortlessly into their theses.

11.5 Capital Allocation as Training

We discussed how intrinsic value investing aligns with management towards efficient capital allocation, delivering resources to the enterprises that will have enduring success. For me, becoming a father drove home both the long-term and short-term thinking required in investing. The word "husband" is the root for "husbandry", emphasizing management and resource conservation. When the best defense is offense, growth indicates good management, just as it is when tending a child. Writ large, investors are capital allocators and stewards of society in the long term. That is the mantle that investors such as Buffett have placed on the generations of investors he has trained. The mantle is the same reason why powerful methods that we've covered must be used to their full capability. Good stewardship frees up resources for the rest of society. It is a competitive vocation, rightly so given its importance.

Stewardship has an ideal personified by the Founding Fathers, who gave a principled approach to governance. In 2022, active management outperformed passive management by a wide margin, revealing how the passive management tide has wrought a more fragile environment.[90] Passive management gained popularity on the general premise that the active fund management business contains an unsound human element. The Founding Fathers, as a group that saw the abuses of Church powers vested in State, understood human failures. They held that the power of government should be derived from the consent of the governed, and that citizens have a right and a duty to participate in the political system. The Founding Fathers promoted the idea of individual rights and personal responsibility. The system of checks and balances is enhanced when active human managers engage with AI systems that compile conversational knowledge across the swath of the business community. Stewardship has the ideal of a progress towards a better outcome.

Blackrock CEO Larry Fink received considerable pushback with its ESG initiatives. In part, ESG had become a culture war symbol. MIT Professor Sandy Pentland, head of the MIT Connection Science program, says that ESG means 200 different things to 200 different people, whereas something as simple as delivering clean drinking water to communities in need is a universal value. As AI value investing enables durable long-term investments, longer time horizons will inevitably converge to universal provisions, such as clean drinking water.

Lofty concepts as stewardship and long-term vision aren't abstract. The legendary Yale endowment manager David Swensen put long-term vision in practice through techniques discussed in his seminal work "Pioneering Portfolio Management: An Unconventional Approach to Institutional Investment". His core proposition echoed that of Keynes' "General Theory". Liquidity preference in asset allocation translates to outperformance. Swensen steered the Yale endowment into timber and hedge funds to great effect, swelling the Yale endowment from $1 Bn to $29 Bn from 1985 to 2019. Amazingly, he took the reins of Yale's endowment at the age of 31. It's a two-fold story of return on investment – Yale's provost recognized that Swensen would emerge as a great steward given responsibility in fashion of Sir Gawain.

Stewardship doesn't mean easy decisions. Buffett demonstrated good stewardship in times of stress when he rescued Salomon Brothers. The biographer Roger Lowenstein writes of Buffett charging into Salomon Brothers to stare the big swinging egos in the eye to curtail their compensation. What a sight it would've been to see the fire in Buffett's eyes as he held the desk, the Buck stops here. Buffett has been hard on the rest of the financial community.

Value investing, by bent of the long-term outlook, is a training ground for stewardship. Stewardship binds individuals and institutions. As Buffett has taught us, it's a philosophy and a discipline. It finds its expression in companies like Nvidia, whose cultural DNA is doing the engineering that others can't or won't. Like investing, companies don't set a limit on the creativity and lengths to which motivated individuals can shape their destiny for better outcomes.

11.6 Conservatism

Conservatism in value investing avoids asset bubbles, like when Buffett shuttered his partnership in 1969 due to frothy public valuations. Remarkably, LLMs used in an ML framework uncover an intrinsic valuation cycle, and support Buffett's ability to gauge bubbles in his comprehensive reading. Value investors represent a powerful contingent in markets, but for better or worse, don't dominate markets. Contrasting Munger and Buffett presents a cautionary tale of respecting Mr. Market in his vagaries.

Unfortunately, Munger wound down his investment partnership in 1975. Munger had followed the later Citi CEO's exasperation, "As long as the music is playing, you've got to get up and dance." The senescence of Blue Chip Stamps rocked Munger's partnership. After shuttering, the partnership between Buffett and Munger has been highly successful, with Munger contributing his unique style of value investing and rational decision-making that we've covered.

We don't fault Munger for staying invested – predicting the madness of men is a monumental task if dancing to the market's beat. Buffett's conservatism in Berkshire checked Munger's demons. Buffett appreciates that cash is king, especially when high interest rates reward the liquidity preference. Buffett uses his liquidity through his exquisite valuation barometer.

The barometer we built shows a cyclical nature to valuations.

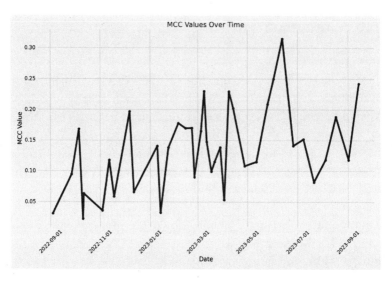

Figure 11.9: Tracking the MCC values (prediction metric) as we bring our latest LLM ensemble online. We continuously improved the AI, which generated the upward trend. However, a pronounced cyclicality is still observed.

We track a correlation coefficient (the MCC) to gauge the performance of our AI and measure the quality of factor prediction. The correlation accounts for true positives, true negatives, false positives, and false negatives. The coefficient ranges from -1 to 1, where 1 represents perfect prediction, 0 represents no better than random prediction, and -1 indicates total disagreement between prediction and observation. Usually in finance, the Information Ratio measures the excess return of a portfolio relative to its benchmark, per unit of active risk taken. A higher Information Ratio indicates that the portfolio manager has generated higher returns without taking on significantly more risk. Both metrics assist in decision-making, albeit in different contexts. MCC helps decide the effectiveness of the AI, while Information Ratio assists in a more direct measurement of the portfolio. Our AI seeks to classify company valuation into performance quintiles on a six month forward-chaining (causal) basis. In fig. 11.9, we show the forward test, meaning the real-time run without model architecture or hyperparameter changes (no p-hacking). Surprisingly, the intrinsic valuation cycles are well-visualized within the overall trend.

A caveat is due to the current version of the AI, there is only a year of history. Nevertheless, it bolsters conviction that alpha hasn't been eroded by competitors. Intrinsic value investing has been valuable since Buffett's start in the Forties. Due to human nature and Mr. Market, value investing will never fall out of favor. Our quantitative results corroborate established wisdom, while perhaps for the first time in history, properly emulating Buffett's methods quantitatively.

11.7 Capital And Labor In the 21st Century

French economist Thomas Piketty's exhaustive study "Capital in the Twenty-First Century" painted a bleak picture. Unexpectedly, generative AI presents a way out of the encroaching forces foreseen by Piketty that entrap global humanity under an unearned oligarchy. While Piketty's work appears an indictment of capitalism, most free world thinkers would at least shudder at the inequities perpetrated by closed societies. A solution must be borne out of values of freedom and liberty that balance labor and capital.

Piketty's exhaustive work focuses on scenarios where return on capital exceeds economic growth, wealth inequality tends to increase, leading to a society dominated more by wealth (and inheritance) than by labor income. In his analysis, World Wars and policy responses to the Great Depression reduced wealth inequality significantly. This was due to physical destruction of capital, high taxes, inflation, and policy decisions. The post-war period saw policies that favored a broader distribution of wealth, but these effects began to reverse by the 1980s.

In recent decades particularly in the US, Piketty highlights the emergence of "super managers." These top-tier executives have seen their compensations skyrocket, often in ways that appear disconnected from their actual productivity or their companies' successes. Such dramatic pay scales have further fueled income inequality.

To counter the perils of growing wealth disparity, Piketty proposes a solution – a global tax on capital. While he acknowledges the myriad political challenges inherent in implementing such a measure, he views it as an essential step in curbing extreme wealth concentration. Transparency and the accessibility of data on income and wealth are central to his arguments. He emphasizes that without such openness, democratic societies might falter. If unchecked, the 21st century could witness wealth disparities echoing the vast differences of the Belle Époque era in Europe.

We've outlined generative AI changing average managers into

the super managers that Piketty highlights (fig. 1.1). The AI methods here are not all confined to investment, and seek to lift the curve of productivity, much in the way that post-war productivity filled demand that had opened. Only a broad democratization of technology can propel American exceptionalism to new heights.

11.8 Deep Strategy

This book instills ML first principles into investing analysis. Best practices elevate great companies, effecting a deep cultural change. These changes aren't minor changes. It penetrates the institutional processes that make habit, destiny. Cumulative habits yield multiplicative effects. Developing valuable AI skills is like Bill Gates working a mainframe as teen – increasingly accessible. Yet the core is already here. The ironic twist is that the most accomplished investors have already internalized that preternatural ability of working "not to fool oneself". The Second Machine Age expounds on the man-machine hybrids:

> Their skill at manipulating and "coaching" their computers to look very deeply into positions effectively counteracted the superior chess understanding of their grandmaster opponents and the greater computational power of other participants. Weak human + machine + better process was superior to a strong computer alone and, more remarkably, superior to a strong human + machine + inferior process.
> – Chapter 12, Learning To Race With Machines

Throughout, we have propounded generative AI as a worthy partner. Like the junior associate, AI must be molded to your processes. Luckily, it is now easier than ever, now AI is now socialized (aligned) and steeped in our traditions. A modern portfolio is a concrete manifestation of the manager's world view. When we discussed drivers of value, the investment manager's values have real social interaction. The AI partner is one that grows from your energy and creativity.

11.9 Our Shared Destiny

My father achieved amazing business success in the face of challenges as a first generation immigrant. While he provided me with a top class education, a system limited my father's advancement, even while his enormous talents lit a fire inside me. My father created a successful business, not once, but twice. The first time he took an offer to move 8000 miles from the emerald bays of Hong Kong to the frigid Bostonian Northeast. There he established the first MetLife branch in New England. His beachhead and charisma jettisoned MetLife into the heart of the AAPI community. As a senior manager, he arduously rehearsed with language coaches on tape to acclimate his accent for corporate boardrooms. Despite his dedication, the corporate world repaid his devotion with a layoff in the late Nineties.

Incredibly, he shrugged off the layoff to start his own competing business while putting three kids through private college. With my mother, they re-enacted Buffett's Mrs. B tale, showing corporate should learn to respect the incredible innovation and hardwork of immigrants that earn every inch. In the twilight of his career, my father turned to managing investments, and there he again encountered his old nemesis. He couldn't master reading the language, the torrential volume required for value investing recommended by Buffett. For Dad, reading 500 pages a day wasn't possible with a second language learned late in life.

Watching my father hit limits made me incredibly angry. As a teenager, I felt intensely angry he was held down by a bamboo ceiling in the corporate world, merely on the basis of his accent.

It made me angry that a company that he had given his decades of loyal service discarded him so quickly during a financial downturn. It angered me when he hadn't the language skills for the closed door politicking so common in Nineties-era boardrooms. It made me angry that my Dad couldn't reach his goals, because the game was rigged against him from the outset. In 2022, my Dad was debilitated by a COVID infection that escalated to sepsis. Nevertheless, my Dad's amazing accomplishments gave me his passion for investment, and that lit a fire in me to develop AI tools in natural language. It's my enduring passion to empower people like my dad with AI.

In my professional capacity, we provided investment research targeting 3000 non-native speakers pro bono. To uplift the community is exactly the spirit that my dad inspired in me when he introduced me to Buffett's writings. Further, his independent streak endures in me as everyday his struggle motivates me.

My dad was a social person and a pillar of the community. New technologies must be ethical and serve marginalized communities.

11.10 The Alignment Problem

Finance and generative AI have the same problem sometimes – they don't do what the designers want. In AI, this is known as the alignment problem and in finance, it's known as systemic risk. Systemic risk occurred in the collateralized debt obligations from so-called financial engineers that while packaged in one way, behaved in another. For generative AI, RLHF has made great strides in aligning generative models to make them useful. With hallucinations and poor calculation, a problem still exists. Simple solutions like averaging five responses isn't the question here. Will we have a system we can rely on?

In finance, regulation has wrought the Common Equity Tier 1

(CET1) regulation. As a standard used to gauge a bank's financial health, it's the core capital of a bank, composed of its most stable and secure financial instruments. CET1 includes the common stock of a bank (ordinary shares), retained earnings, and comprehensive income. It excludes preferred stock and minority interests that don't pass loss absorbency criteria. Namely, CET1 should grow ever year (some headed north of 13%) and bankers like JP Morgan's Dimon chafe at its restrictions. Yet, CET1 exists to curb the bad behavior prevalent in finance. It establishes buffers such that taxpayers aren't footing the bill when should've known better bankers jointly confess their transgressions.

The AI problem has a certain equivalent of CET1 currently. The hardware to support powerful AI is costly and power hungry. Such asset requirements serve as a hurdle to limit bad actors, but the bulwark won't last forever. Nvidia drives performance per energy unit to new heights every year. Only when an equivalent to absorb AI risk for agents – an agent liability, will the AI alignment have open society regulation.

11.11 AI Ethics and Responsible Investment

AI and ML tools can link environmental safety and governance to corporate performance. In our study on Carbon Disclosure Project natural language survey, we teased out just that. Specifically, we investigated ML approaches to understand corporate performance in relation to environmental and social issues. We've used the data provided by the Carbon Disclosure Project (CDP), a non-profit organization that collects environmental data from companies and cities across the world.

From a global dataset, we collated data looking specifically at things like a city's exposure to climate hazards, the steps they've taken to prepare for these risks, and the amount of money they're spending on climate initiatives. We used these factors to create a score for each city that indicates their adaptability to climate change. Additionally, we examined the role of companies in these cities, creating an index that measures their influence on a city's adaptability. In particular, we looked at how a corporation's actions can affect a city's climate resilience both now and in the future.

New York City (NYC) stood out for having corporations that were actively mitigating their environmental impact. Intriguingly, NYC, the global hub for blue chip corporations, is leading the charge in corporate environmental responsibility. NYC-based corporations are particularly proactive when it comes to mitigating their environmental impact. This includes reducing their carbon footprint, utilizing more sustainable materials in their supply chains, and transitioning to renewable energy sources for their operations.

A prime example of such a practice comes from the city's finance sector. Major banks and asset management firms are actively channeling funds into renewable energy projects. Their financial support is not just limited to solar and wind power initiatives, but includes other innovative technologies aimed at reducing carbon emissions and environmental degradation.

Tech and media companies in the City have started introducing energy-saving policies. Corporations like Google are making a conscious effort to decrease their overall energy consumption, and many have committed to powering their operations entirely with renewable energy sources, such as solar or wind power. Retail companies form another large segment of NYC's corporate landscape. Many of these businesses have shifted towards more sustainable practices, such as using recyclable materials for packaging, and promoting products that have been ethically sourced and produced. Some of these companies are also taking active steps to ensure they're providing their employees and customers

City	Exposure	Marginal Corporate Adaptability
NYC	20356	1656.2
Indianapolis	776	605.4
Phoenix	1890	54.0
Philadelphia	832	53.6
Seattle	1872	23.2
Dallas	3240	-86.4
Houston	10870	-352.9
Columbus	3540	-12753.8

Figure 11.10: Marginal corporate adaptability (effect of corporations) on cities according to our custom metrics. Full code is available.[91]

with access to clean drinking water, as a way of further demonstrating their commitment to sustainable practices.

Such corporate initiatives have significantly boosted NYC's adaptability score (fig. 11.10). By focusing on the marginal contribution of corporations to a city's adaptability, we gain insights into potential avenues for mitigation and the impacts of economic actors on climate change. This holistic approach is key to understanding the multi-faceted nature of climate change and the paths towards sustainability. The final score is a measure of a city's preparedness for climate change, factoring in its capacity to reduce greenhouse gas emissions, adapt to changing environmental conditions, and recover from climate-related disasters.

By actively reducing their environmental impact, these corporations are not only safeguarding their own future, but they're also contributing to the overall resilience of the city. This collaboration between NYC and its corporations is a prime example of how sustainability and business can go hand-in-hand. The practices implemented here could serve as a model for other corporations and cities worldwide, helping them enhance their adaptability in the face of climate change. Combined with the tailwind from the Inflation Reduction Act for infrastructure investment, adaptability is bound to rise to new heights.

We also examined companies in energy-intensive industries and their potential impact on climate damage. By transforming descriptions of their actions into quantifiable data, we analyzed their performance to consider the effects of their operations on the environment.

Finally, we used AI to understand the relationship between topics discussed in the data to calculate the collaboration strength between cities and companies. This is a measure of how closely a company's environmental efforts align with the environmental needs of the city it is based in.

Our work reveals the complex interplay between corporations, cities, and the environment, and underscores the important role that businesses can play in making our cities more resilient to climate change. We blend AI, environmental science, and economics to provide a fresh and transparent perspective on sustainable investing.

11.12 Revolutionary Groundwork

We closed the first chapter with the controversial figure of Paracelsus, an alchemist, empiricist, and physician. Unexpectedly, those who wander and question like Paracelsus provide an instrumental role in the development of technique. In Thomas Kuhn's "Structure of Scientific Revolutions", he coined the term paradigm shift to describe the punctuated equilibrium of progress. In his objectivist view, he concentrates on phenomena that precipitates a scientific revolution, like arc minutes of light curving around the moon's gravity well cementing general relativity's prominence. Kuhn doesn't elaborate the human element in his first presentation.

Yet we must necessarily take up the human element in investing as it's complexity personified. Investors are wrapped up in their own mental perceptions as much as language forms perception. Figures like Paracelsus emerge as harbingers of a scientific revolution. His biographer Philip Ball writes:

> Before the fertile logic of a genuinely scientific rationalism could assert itself, the sterile ground of Classical dogma had to give way to a form of empiricism that accepted the reality of certain unknowns and inexplicables... In this sense, men like Paracelsus and his fellow iconoclast Cornelius Agrippa were skeptics: they were prepared, indeed determined, to question what had gone before, to find things out for themselves rather than taking someone else's word for it. [92]

Paracelsus senses with emerging technique, we must grow unsettled with the paradigms of the past. In our presentation, we've taken entirely a scientific and evidence-based approach. We're driven by an uncomfortable urge that the new techniques of the age must unify with our growing skill for a stronger pursuit. The broad democratic basis of AI gives us a technique meant to embody the best of our collective power. For a democratic technology, we must all shoulder Paracelsus' mantle, in the face of certain unknowns, to usher in a better age.

Acknowledgements

The creation of a comprehensive view is the result of many mentors and editors along the way. The author would like to thank the following: his parents, Daniel Mahoney, Wayne Tam, Myles Thompson, Ayesha Rafi, Neel Patel, Michael Lapat, Fausto Milletari, Henry Lin, Greg Peterfreund, Edward Zhang, Jensen Huang, Kay Giesecke, Stu Woo, Nick Haber, Yuji Kosugi, Jason Su, Barrett Williams, Michael Wang, Regina Wang, his in-laws, Apaar Sadhwani, Naeem Zafar, David Nola, Cassandra Carothers, Jon Lunetta, Rakesh Mathur, Catalin Voss, Calvin Ho, reiterate the numerous teachers mentioned in the text, and many, many, many others.

Of course, we offer a special acknowledgement for Buffett and Munger. To the loudest of the Silent Generation – whence we'd go without the wisdom of the generations?

We thank the developers and contributors of archive.is. Many bibliographic links direct there to avoid the frustrating effects of link rot. If the original link is still live, it is readily regenerated.

And finally, thank you to you, the reader. Please consider leaving a review if you enjoyed the text, and subscribing for updates at amicusai.substack.com.

About the Author

Leonidas is the Co-Founder and Managing Partner of Amicus Investments, an ML research and advisory firm. He is a seasoned leader in AI, having founded and launched the NVIDIA Deep Learning Institute, the global educational and professional development organization. Previously, he was a Senior Research Scientist at NVIDIA and a research scientist at Stanford University Department of Radiology.

At Stanford, he demonstrated outstanding performance in competitions, placing in the top 3% of a competition sponsored by the California Healthcare Foundation, and securing second place in a commodities trading contest. He holds multiple patents in deep learning and machine learning. He lives with his wife and daughter in Silicon Valley. He earned his BSc in Mathematics-Physics from Brown University and Engineering PhD from Yale University.

Bibliography

[1] Michael Lewis. *Flash boys: a Wall Street revolt*. WW Norton & Company, 2014.

[2] https://archive.ph/yarhu.

[3] https://archive.ph/x762p.

[4] Gregory Zuckerman. *The man who solved the market: How Jim Simons launched the quant revolution*. Penguin, 2019.

[5] Philip A Fisher. *Common stocks and uncommon profits and other writings*, volume 40. John Wiley & Sons, 2003.

[6] https://xkcd.com/1425/.

[7] Alex Krizhevsky, Ilya Sutskever, and Geoffrey E Hinton. Imagenet classification with deep convolutional neural networks. *Communications of the ACM*, 60(6):84–90, 2017.

[8] https://super.gluebenchmark.com/.

[9] Kiyosi Itô. Memoirs of my research on stochastic analysis. In *Proc. The Abel Symp. 2005, Stochastic Anal. Appl.-A Symposium in Honor of Kiyosi Ito-*. Citeseer, 2007.

[10] William F Sharpe. Capital asset prices: A theory of market equilibrium under conditions of risk. *The journal of finance*, 19(3):425–442, 1964.

[11] Tianqi Chen, Tong He, Michael Benesty, Vadim Khotilovich, Yuan Tang, Hyunsu Cho, Kailong Chen, Rory Mitchell, Ignacio Cano, Tianyi Zhou, et al. Xgboost: extreme gradient boosting. *R package version 0.4-2*, 1(4):1–4, 2015.

[12] Anton Maximilian Schäfer and Hans-Georg Zimmermann. Recurrent neural networks are universal approximators. *International journal of neural systems*, 17(04):253–263, 2007.

[13] https://graphics.stanford.edu/projects/brookgpu/.

[14] https://archive.ph/mgatx.

[15] https://www.sec.gov/edgar/filer-information/past-edgar-technical-specifications.

[16] Talia Gillis, Bryce McLaughlin, and Jann Spiess. On the fairness of machine-assisted human decisions. *arXiv preprint arXiv:2110.15310*, 2021.

[17] Leo K Tam, Xiaosong Wang, and Daguang Xu. Transformer query-target knowledge discovery (tend): drug discovery from cord-19. *arXiv preprint arXiv:2012.04682*, 2020.

[18] Jonathan Krause, Benjamin Sapp, Andrew Howard, Howard Zhou, Alexander Toshev, Tom Duerig, James Philbin, and Li Fei-Fei. The unreasonable effectiveness of noisy data for fine-grained recognition. In *Computer Vision–ECCV 2016: 14th European Conference, Amsterdam, The Netherlands, October 11-14, 2016, Proceedings, Part III 14*, pages 301–320. Springer, 2016.

[19] David Thissen, Lynne Steinberg, and Daniel Kuang. Quick and easy implementation of the benjamini-hochberg procedure for controlling the false positive rate in multiple com-

parisons. *Journal of educational and behavioral statistics*, 27(1):77–83, 2002.

[20] https://archive.ph/pvj09.

[21] Harry Markowitz. Portfolio selection. *The Journal of Finance*, 7(1):77–91, 1952.

[22] https://x.com/economyapp/status/1694448140336984537?s=20.

[23] John L Kelly. A new interpretation of information rate. *the bell system technical journal*, 35(4):917–926, 1956.

[24] Dražen Prelec, H Sebastian Seung, and John McCoy. A solution to the single-question crowd wisdom problem. *Nature*, 541(7638):532–535, 2017.

[25] Jonathan Haskel and Stian Westlake. *Capitalism without capital: The rise of the intangible economy.* Princeton University Press, 2018.

[26] John C Bogle. *The little book of common sense investing: the only way to guarantee your fair share of stock market returns.* John Wiley & Sons, 2017.

[27] https://archive.ph/tx4ag.

[28] https://archive.ph/m2nla.

[29] https://archive.ph/ior3u.

[30] https://archive.ph/4y4ja.

[31] https://press.spglobal.com/2022-03-04-s-p-dow-jones-indices-announces-update-to-s-p-composite-1500-market-cap-guidelines.

[32] Benjamin Franklin. *The Autobiography of Benjamin Franklin*, volume 41. PF Collier, 1909.

[33] Cal Newport. *Deep work: Rules for focused success in a distracted world.* Hachette UK, 2016.

[34] https://www.dataroma.com/m/stock.php?sym=mu.

[35] Ludwig Wittgenstein. *Philosophical investigations.* §630. 2019.

[36] https://seekingalpha.com/article/4618353-taiwan-semiconductor-manufacturing-company-limited-tsm-q2-2023-earnings-call-transcript?source=content$_{type}$

[37] Vahe Tshitoyan, John Dagdelen, Leigh Weston, Alexander Dunn, Ziqin Rong, Olga Kononova, Kristin A Persson, Gerbrand Ceder, and Anubhav Jain. Unsupervised word embeddings capture latent knowledge from materials science literature. *Nature,* 571(7763):95–98, 2019.

[38] https://www.wsj.com/articles/louis-a-simpson-once-seen-as-warren-buffetts-successor-dies-at-age-85-11642518001.

[39] https://archive.ph/uvcwf.

[40] https://www.youtube.com/watch?v=$_{e}wkal7s3g$.

[41] Aye M Soe. Low-volatility portfolio construction: ranking versus optimization. *The Journal of Beta Investment Strategies,* 3(3):63–73, 2012.

[42] https://www.youtube.com/watch?v=rgggoccmeiyfeature=youtu.be.

[43] Maohao Shen, Yuheng Bu, Prasanna Sattigeri, Soumya Ghosh, Subhro Das, and Gregory Wornell. Post-hoc uncertainty learning using a dirichlet meta-model. In *Proceedings of the AAAI Conference on Artificial Intelligence,* volume 37, pages 9772–9781, 2023.

[44] https://archive.ph/tosya.

[45] Leonard Salewski, Stephan Alaniz, Isabel Rio-Torto, Eric Schulz, and Zeynep Akata. In-context impersonation reveals large language models' strengths and biases. *arXiv preprint arXiv:2305.14930*, 2023.

[46] Sang Michael Xie, Aditi Raghunathan, Percy Liang, and Tengyu Ma. An explanation of in-context learning as implicit bayesian inference. *arXiv preprint arXiv:2111.02080*, 2021.

[47] https://archive.ph/5hefw.

[48] Chip Heath and Dan Heath. *Made to stick: Why some ideas survive and others die.* Random House, 2007.

[49] Stephanie Chan, Adam Santoro, Andrew Lampinen, Jane Wang, Aaditya Singh, Pierre Richemond, James McClelland, and Felix Hill. Data distributional properties drive emergent in-context learning in transformers. *Advances in Neural Information Processing Systems*, 35:18878–18891, 2022.

[50] Dmitrii Krasheninnikov, Egor Krasheninnikov, and David Krueger. Out-of-context meta-learning in large language models. In *ICLR 2023 Workshop on Mathematical and Empirical Understanding of Foundation Models*, 2023.

[51] Wes Gurnee and Max Tegmark. Language models represent space and time. *arXiv preprint arXiv:2310.02207*, 2023.

[52] https://archive.ph/jvl7r.

[53] Nisan Stiennon, Long Ouyang, Jeffrey Wu, Daniel Ziegler, Ryan Lowe, Chelsea Voss, Alec Radford, Dario Amodei, and Paul F Christiano. Learning to summarize with human feedback. *Advances in Neural Information Processing Systems*, 33:3008–3021, 2020.

[54] Alec Radford, Jeffrey Wu, Rewon Child, David Luan, Dario Amodei, Ilya Sutskever, et al. Language models are unsupervised multitask learners. *OpenAI blog*, 1(8):9, 2019.

[55] Long Ouyang, Jeffrey Wu, Xu Jiang, Diogo Almeida, Carroll Wainwright, Pamela Mishkin, Chong Zhang, Sandhini Agarwal, Katarina Slama, Alex Ray, et al. Training language models to follow instructions with human feedback. *Advances in Neural Information Processing Systems*, 35:27730–27744, 2022.

[56] https://archive.ph/ainwa.

[57] Leo Gao, Stella Biderman, Sid Black, Laurence Golding, Travis Hoppe, Charles Foster, Jason Phang, Horace He, Anish Thite, Noa Nabeshima, et al. The pile: An 800gb dataset of diverse text for language modeling. *arXiv preprint arXiv:2101.00027*, 2020.

[58] https://www.redditinc.com/blog/reddits-2019-year-in-review/.

[59] Michael J Frank and David Badre. Mechanisms of hierarchical reinforcement learning in corticostriatal circuits 1: computational analysis. *Cerebral cortex*, 22(3):509–526, 2012.

[60] https://archive.ph/coccs.

[61] David Badre and Michael J Frank. Mechanisms of hierarchical reinforcement learning in cortico–striatal circuits 2: Evidence from fmri. *Cerebral cortex*, 22(3):527–536, 2012.

[62] Jane X Wang, Zeb Kurth-Nelson, Dharshan Kumaran, Dhruva Tirumala, Hubert Soyer, Joel Z Leibo, Demis Hassabis, and Matthew Botvinick. Prefrontal cortex as a meta-reinforcement learning system. *Nature neuroscience*, 21(6):860–868, 2018.

[63] Jane X Wang, Michael King, Nicolas Porcel, Zeb Kurth-Nelson, Tina Zhu, Charlie Deck, Peter Choy, Mary Cassin, Malcolm

Reynolds, Francis Song, et al. Alchemy: A benchmark and analysis toolkit for meta-reinforcement learning agents. *arXiv preprint arXiv:2102.02926*, 2021.

[64] https://archive.ph/rrv36.

[65] https://www.statista.com/statistics/272028/poker-players-worldwide-since-2006-according-to-origin/.

[66] https://archive.ph/zfx6j.

[67] https://www.youtube.com/watch?v=oo-akx66i24.

[68] https://archive.ph/7oerr.

[69] https://fortune.com/2015/12/29/hedge-funds-fortune-1966/.

[70] https://archive.ph/m1mgy.

[71] https://archive.ph/o1fjb.

[72] https://archive.ph/yupul.

[73] William Poundstone. *Fortune's formula: The untold story of the scientific betting system that beat the casinos and Wall Street.* Hill and Wang, 2010.

[74] Kailas Vodrahalli, Tobias Gerstenberg, and James Y Zou. Uncalibrated models can improve human-ai collaboration. *Advances in Neural Information Processing Systems*, 35:4004–4016, 2022.

[75] https://quac.ai/.

[76] Aarohi Srivastava, Abhinav Rastogi, Abhishek Rao, Abu Awal Md Shoeb, Abubakar Abid, Adam Fisch, Adam R Brown, Adam Santoro, Aditya Gupta, Adrià Garriga-Alonso, et al. Beyond the imitation game: Quantifying and extrapolating the capabilities of language models. *arXiv preprint arXiv:2206.04615*, 2022.

[77] Isaac Kauvar, Chris Doyle, Linqi Zhou, and Nick Haber. Curious replay for model-based adaptation. 2023.

[78] Jonathan Frankle and Michael Carbin. The lottery ticket hypothesis: Finding sparse, trainable neural networks. *arXiv preprint arXiv:1803.03635*, 2018.

[79] Chunyuan Li, Heerad Farkhoor, Rosanne Liu, and Jason Yosinski. Measuring the intrinsic dimension of objective landscapes. *arXiv preprint arXiv:1804.08838*, 2018.

[80] Deborah A Small, George Loewenstein, and Paul Slovic. Can insight breed callousness? the impact of learning about the identifiable victim effect on sympathy. *Unpublished manuscript*, 2005.

[81] https://archive.ph/vbq5y.

[82] Sheena Iyengar. *Think Bigger: How to Innovate*. Columbia University Press, 2023.

[83] OpenAI. Gpt-4 technical report, 2023.

[84] https://archive.ph/quv1c.

[85] Petter Kolm and Gordon Ritter. On the bayesian interpretation of black–litterman. *European Journal of Operational Research*, 258(2):564–572, 2017.

[86] Nikhil Agarwal, Alex Moehring, Pranav Rajpurkar, and Tobias Salz. Combining human expertise with artificial intelligence: experimental evidence from radiology. Technical report, National Bureau of Economic Research, 2023.

[87] Ozge Akinci, Gianluca Benigno, Serra Pelin, and Jonathan Turek. The dollar's imperial circle. *FRB of New York Staff Report*, (1045), 2022.

[88] https://archive.ph/5zopz.

[89] Kaiyu Yang, Aidan M Swope, Alex Gu, Rahul Chalamala, Peiyang Song, Shixing Yu, Saad Godil, Ryan Prenger, and Anima Anandkumar. Leandojo: Theorem proving with retrieval-augmented language models. *arXiv preprint arXiv:2306.15626*, 2023.

[90] https://www.wsj.com/articles/big-hedge-funds-are-top-performers-for-a-change-11674094967.

[91] https://archive.ph/ckujf.

[92] Philip Ball. *The devil's doctor: Paracelsus and the world of Renaissance magic and science.* Random House, 2014.

Index